LAMBORGHINI
Supercar Supreme

BY THE AUTO EDITORS OF CONSUMER GUIDE®

PUBLICATIONS INTERNATIONAL, LTD.

CREDITS

OWNERS
Special thanks to the owners of the cars featured in this book
for their enthusiastic cooperation. They are listed below, with
the page number(s) on which their cars appear.
Mike Brady: 19, 21, 22. Bruce Canepa: 65, 83. Bernie Chase: 18,
21, 23, 56, 58. Steve Doley: 59. Ron Fair: 26, 27. Gil & Vicki
Gilfix: 37, 38, 39. David Green: 32, 33. Mark Griffith: 20, 22. Jim
Kaminski: 75. Jack Kellham: 9, 13, 14. L&L International: 60,
62. Danny Latner: 41, 43. William Locke: 46, 47. Raymond
Maranges: 52, 53. Motortech Inc: 64. Al & Lois Parodi: 44, 45.
A.J. Pegno: 81. David Piangerelli: 5, 14, 15, 16. Dr. S. Radtke:
49. Albert Romvari: 78, 79. Jack Rosenzweig: 74. Rick Schans:
79. Tony Voiture: 25. Harry Woodnorth: 30.

PHOTO CREDITS
The editors would like to thank the following people for sup-
plying the photography that made this book possible. They are
listed below, along with the page number(s) of their photos.
Albert Porter: 9, 13. Franco Zagari: 12, 17, 18, 29, 36, 42, 48, 56.
Neil Doherty: 5, 14, 15, 16, 32, 33. Dennis Doty: 14. J.F.
Marchet: 14. Vince Manocchi: 18, 21, 23, 56, 58. Nicky Wright:
19, 21, 22, 74, 79. Jim Thompson: 20, 22. Thomas Glatch: 25.
David Gooley: 26, 27, 59. *Carrozzeria Bertone SpA*: 29. Sam
Griffith: 30. Mirco DeCet: 7, 30, 31, 43, 50, 71, 75, 82, 83, 85, 86,
88, 89, 90, 91, 92–93, 94–95. Franco Rossi: 36. Bud Juneau: 37,
38, 39, 44, 45, 78, 79. Jerry Heasley: 41, 43. Zoom
Photographics: 39, 46, 47, 75. John Owens: 49. Ken
Beebe/Kugler Studio: 60, 62. Sam Griffith: 64, 83. Tom
McClellan: 65. Scott Rosenberg: 81. White Eagle Studio: 86, 87.

Very special thanks to: Sandro Munari, Technical/Public
Relations, *Automobili Lamborghini SpA*. Joseph Hannah,
President of Lamborghini, USA. Tony Cervone, Chrysler Corp.
Public Relations. Dr. Gian Beppe Panicco, *Carrozzeria Bertone
SpA*.

CONTENTS

A MAN AND HIS DREAM

FROM THE UNGAINLY 350 GTV

TO THE SHOW STOPPING DIABLO,

LAMBORGHINIS HAVE ALWAYS

HAD SOMETHING SPECIAL. WHAT

THEY HAVE IS THE HEART AND

SOUL OF FOUNDER FERRUCCIO.

Today the supercar market is crowded with pretenders. Makers like McLaren, Yamaha, and Acura, squeeze the elite market. What these newcomers—and their cars—lack is a sense of history, or character if you will. Though their automobiles might be technically advanced, stunningly styled, or blindingly fast, they will never have the emotional appeal of the cars created by Ferruccio Lamborghini.

Life at Sant'Agata is vastly different from what it was 30 short years ago. In November of 1993, parent-owner Chrysler, sold *Automobili Lamborghini SpA* to MegaTech Ltd.—a holding company 100 percent owned by SEDTCO Pty., an Indonesian conglomerate. Changes like this are nothing new to Lamborghini. In fact, the company has gone through several financial crises and ownership changes in the 20-or-so years since Ferruccio sold out to a Swiss watchmaker. Lamborghini was even operated by the Italian government for a while. Yet one thing will always remain—from the original 350 GTV to the super fast Diablo SE30—the cars were the subject of Ferruccio's dream and desire to build the best.

He was born on April 28, 1916, which made him a Taurus. That may not have had anything to do with his character, but he clearly perceived that it did. Individuals born under the sign of the bull are said to be winners; aggressive and goal-oriented, determined to achieve material success and social dominance through initiative, tenacity, and hard work. This is the substance of Ferruccio's life's work.

Ferruccio was born on April 28, 1916, making him a Taurus. He believed that was a sign, and the charging bull came to symbolize Lamborghini.

The Lamborghinis were farmers, stolid peasant folk of the flat, fertile fields of the broad Po valley, so stocky little Ferruccio grew up with his feet in the soil. But this was the automotive century and, like numerous other youngsters of that time and place, he had motor oil in his veins. Machinery of every type fascinated him, and he was not immune to the enthusiasm for fast cars that made Italy a major power in European auto racing during his boyhood. While he was still a boy, Ferruccio is said to have set up a primitive but workable machine shop, forge, and casting foundry in the family barn. The story even has his enterprise once setting fire to the structure.

Acknowledging their son's talents and ambitions, Ferruccio's parents packed him off for formal technical schooling in the nearby "big city" of Bologna, where he reportedly earned an industrial arts degree. After that, young Lamborghini apprenticed himself to a Bologna mechanical shop.

World War II might have derailed his career, as it did for so many. However, the *Regia Aeronautica* stationed Ferruccio at a base on the island of Rhodes, off the Turkish coast, and put him to work in the transport pool. Rhodes was not a theater of heavy action, but neither was it at the top of the military's list for replacement equipment. Lamborghini soon became known as something of a wizard at keeping decrepit vehicles running.

One tale has Lamborghini making an "improvement" to the braking system of his commanding officer's cherished Alfa—which promptly sent the car into the Mediterranean. It might have sent Ferruccio to the stockade, but he seemed to have the kind of personality that made even COs grin.

After the war, Lamborghini's hands naturally fell on mechanic's tools again, and now his parents' investment in his education was repaid. Like other farmers in the region, they were in urgent need of a new tractor, but there was no hope of obtaining one in postwar Italy. No problem. Their son duly built them one—out of junk.

There is a story that Ferruccio got the idea for this on his wedding trip. British forces in Italy were disposing of a small fleet of light armored cars, and the happy couple somehow stumbled across them. Needless to say, the bride found her honeymoon at an abrupt end. Whisked home early, she watched as her ambitious, determined new husband tore the armor plate off each car and turned it into a little tractor— a *carioche* in the local vernacular.

Lamborghini's little garage business grew to the point that by 1949 he could erect a new, specially designed factory at Cento. Three years later he was able to start building proper, all-new tractors using two-, three-, and four-cylinder diesel engines of his own design and manufacture. Then, in 1954, Lamborghini scored a first in his field by launching a line of air-cooled, direct-injection diesel tractors. Soon, his *Lamborghini Trattrice* was one of Italy's largest tractor makers and Ferruccio was a wealthy man—respected and honored, and with the financial means to pursue new challenges.

He didn't take long to find them. During a trip to America as part of an Italian trade delegation, Ferruccio came across an idea. In 1960 he duly established *Lamborghini Bruciatori*, in nearby Pieve di Cento, to turn out home and commercial heating and cooling equipment. Ferruccio tackled this second business with characteristic energy and enterprise. For example, he pleased customers with an innovative service plan. He also pleased both his country and his accountants by setting up the business in an economically depressed area. The Italian government was itself an investor.

Lamborghini certainly could have

been satisfied with his first two commercial empires and called it a career as early as 1962. But he had another itch to scratch.

In Italy, the passion for fast driving is as abundant as grapes on hillsides. In setting up as a *trasformatore*, Ferruccio involved himself in a postwar hot-rodding movement that signaled Italy's return to sports-car racing. A mainstay of this impatient little industry was Fiat's 500 Topolino. The beloved "mouse" was a simple, sturdy

In 1963 Lamborghini previewed the 350 GTV at the Turin show. The car that came from that was the 350 GT (*top*). It was Ferruccio's (*left*) dream of the perfect GT car. Just ten years later, the Countach shocked the world with its futuristic styling and angular lines.

baby-car introduced in 1936. It was to become as important to its country's performance enthusiasts as Ford's Model T had been to America's a couple of decades before.

Installing a new overhead-valve cylinder head in a cut-down Topolino, Lamborghini set out to compete in the 1948 running of the classic Mille Miglia road race. He crashed after completing about three-quarters of the near 1000-mile distance. Ferruccio described this incident to a journalist years later: "I finished my Mille Miglia in an osteria (an inn), which I entered by driving though a wall." Neither he nor his co-driver was hurt. It would be Ferruccio's last race.

According to an oft-told tale, there came a day when Ferruccio grew so annoyed with a particular Ferrari that he drove over to Enzo's factory at Maranello. There he tried to get in to complain to the proprietor himself, only to be turned away. No doubt Lamborghini was rebuffed. More than

The car that changed the future of Lamborghini began as a one-off chassis at the 1965 Turin show. The race-car-like frame (*left*) of what would become the beautiful Miura offered a mid-mounted V-12 and a revolutionary chassis layout. Ferruccio (*center*) was a proud man who could often be found on the factory floor working on a car.

very straightforward person. He's always been very honest and very fair."

These engagingly human traits, and simple taurine vigor and audacity, were irresistible to young people of talent and ambition. Infused with creative fervor, they flocked to the heady, free-wheeling climate that surrounded the new *Automobili Ferruccio Lamborghini*. Four in particular would prove to be key figures in the development of Lamborghini cars.

Prime among them is Wallace. As chief development driver, he was ultimately responsible for the performance, road manners, flavor—in a word, the personality—of every Lamborghini automobile.

Born in 1938 outside Auckland, New Zealand, Wallace grew up as much a gearhead as Ferruccio himself, and more of a racer. He says now that he'd been dreaming of joining the Italian auto racing world since he was 10 years old, but it wasn't until he reached 21 that he got on a boat and did it. That was 1959. Over the next four racing seasons he spent time as a factory mechanic with both Ferrari and Maserati, plus a couple of privateer teams. "In late '63, October or November, I had the choice of rejoining Ferrari or taking this job at Lamborghini as mechanic and troubleshooter. I thought there was much more opportunity to learn something there, and I took it."

One of the men Wallace would learn from was a year younger than himself—a gifted 24-year-old engineer named Giampaolo Dallara. Born in a mountain village above Parma into a well-to-do family (his father was the village's mayor), Dallara earned a degree in aeronautical engineering at the Technical Institute of Milan. Thanks to one of his professors, who moonlighted as an engine-design consultant to Ferrari, Dallara bypassed aviation upon graduating and went straight into the automobile business. After 18 months as assistant to then-

a few important visitors to Maranello—including some who'd been invited—have told bitterly of cooling their heels for hours in a narrow anteroom outside *Il Commendatore's* office. It would also have been entirely in character for Ferruccio to drive away in a fury. The successful major industrialist and self-made millionaire resolved that he could damn well build a better car than any of them.

Ferruccio had never been one to let a good story die in the telling. But Bob Wallace, the racing mechanic from New Zealand who was soon to become an integral part of Lamborghini's entire automotive operation, dismisses this bit of folklore with a snort: "Naw, that's all BS, which he himself may have helped keep alive, but nothing like that really happened. What motivated him was prestige, plus the fact he thought he could make money at it."

All that remained was to follow the formula that had already built two manufacturing empires. Accordingly, Ferruccio bought a piece of land and erected a new purpose-built factory. He filled it with the absolute state-of-the-art in automaking equipment and hired the best people in the automotive business.

Upon visiting his new car factory, you'd likely discover, as did American journalist Pete Coltrin, Lamborghini down on the shop floor in shirt-sleeves, happily wrenching away at an engine with employees. People found him an unusually democratic chief executive, one uncommonly willing to delegate authority. This last trait was particularly significant. Said Bob Wallace: "Lamborghini's the typical farmer. He'd say 'Hi' to the president of Italy. He doesn't stand on ceremony. He's, uh, a little crude sometimes, but a very,

Probably the two most outrageous vehicles of the 1980s, the Countach and the LM002 (*right*). What the Countach couldn't do on the road the LM002 could do off. Bertone's Carabo show car (*below*), designed by Marcello Gandini, was a prelude to the Countach.

Ferrari engineer Carlo Chiti, he moved to Maserati to work with his cousin, Giulio Alfieri, before harking to Lamborghini's siren song in March '62. (Years later, Alfieri would also leave the trident for the bull.)

With Dallara, whom Ferruccio named chief engineer, came another young Maserati engineer, Paolo Stanzani. Then 25, he hailed from Bologna. Wallace, who'd previously worked with him at Maserati, says of Stanzani: "He comes from a fairly lower-income family. He struggled his way through the university and that sort of thing. He's always been very bright as an engineer. I think, theoretically, Stanzani might be the brighter one of the two." Stanzani would come to play two key roles at Lamborghini: factory manager and chief engineer.

Rounding out this formidable foursome was Giotto Bizzarrini. Then 36, he had an engineering degree from the University of Pisa and was already well established in Italian performance circles. He had just left Ferrari, where he'd been project director for one of Enzo's most memorable cars, the

immortal 250 GTO that was just being introduced in 1962. He'd also spent time at Alfa Romeo.

Bizzarrini had brought along plans for a new V-12 engine and, like the others had a burning desire: he wanted Lamborghini to go racing.

"I hoped they would," admits Wallace. "Because I personally firmly believe that, for a factory of that type, racing does help the natural overall development of this type of car. So there was always the hope that we would. But the only sane person of all of us, initially, was Lamborghini himself. He said no. And he was right. To have divided things up at that stage would have been sheer insanity."

Still, Ferruccio seems to have been an almost magically fun employer. As

Wallace remembers: "He had an enormous personal interest in the first years, before all the union trouble. That's what really got the company going, because people would work 'til 9, 10, 11 at night. It wasn't a question of money or overtime pay or anything like that. No, everyone was motivated, everyone had a lot of enthusiasm. He'd get stuck in and work too."

On February 20, 1993, Ferruccio Lamborghini died of a heart attack, but he has left a gift with us. It is his cars. The Miura was probably the most beautiful and exciting mid-engined sports car ever produced, and the Diablo is downright devious. These machines will forever hold the heritage that Ferruccio has left us, no matter who owns the company.

CHAPTER ONE

THE EARLY YEARS

FERRUCCIO'S FIRST ATTEMPT

AT THE PERFECT AUTOMOBILE

WAS FAR FROM FLAWLESS.

HOWEVER, THAT CAR'S

SUCCESSOR, THE 350 GT,

WAS A SOLID CAR AROUND

WHICH LAMBORGHINI

WOULD BUILD A LEGEND.

As Lamborghini soon found out, building the best luxury sports car in the world was not as easy as converting old military vehicles into tractors. October of 1963 was fast approaching, and Ferruccio and his talented team were frantically working on completing a car for the Turin auto show.

That car was the 350 GTV. But by the time the show rolled around the GTV was clearly unrefined in design and hastily built. It contained no engine. Though there was some interest, the reviews were bad and public reception was even worse. The debacle probably would have snuffed out the chances of anyone with smaller dreams... or thinner resources.

Lamborghini was as image-conscious as any automaker, so it's difficult to fathom just why he unveiled his first effort before it was complete. (He would do this time and again in subsequent years.) Perhaps he felt pressured to get income flowing. Bob Wallace points out: "Your appearance at a major auto show is worth millions in publicity value." Whatever the reason, the GTV's premature showing must have done some harm from a commercial standpoint.

Ferruccio had gone into the automobile business to realize a dream: a GT "without faults," he had said, "a perfect car." It was hardly that, but the GTV ("V" for *veloce*: fast) oozed excitement, enthusiasm, and ambition. Lamborghini simply couldn't wait to show

it off, a feeling he hoped car enthusiasts everywhere would understand.

There were certain obstacles to overcome. First, just how would you design a "perfect" GT in 1963? Secondly, what was out there to improve upon?

Actually, the opposition was not vast. The main players in this game were those two already great Italian marques, Ferrari and Maserati. Each offered two-seaters and 2+2s that were spacious and plush enough to be comfortable on long trips, fast enough to shorten those trips significantly, and costly enough to make one's arrival an event. Mid-year brought a new Aston Martin from England, the DB5, complete with lightweight *Superleggera* bodywork by Touring of Italy.

As for the other direct competition, it was scarce. Alfa Romeo, Lancia, Jaguar with its curvaceous E-type, Mercedes, Porsche, Chevrolet with its new '63 Corvette Sting Ray, and perhaps Carroll Shelby with his Cobra were all making worthy high-performance cars. However, none had the blend of size, speed, refinement, and sex appeal that spoke to Ferruccio Lamborghini.

Therefore, Ferrari was naturally his main target. Enzo Ferrari, then 65, had devoted much of his life to racing. He'd been a driver in the 1920s and manager of the great independent Scuderia Ferrari team that carried Alfa's banner in the '30s. Ferrari's company, in nearby Maranello, had, since the late '40s, been turning out a broad spectrum of

pure racers and track-tuned sports cars. However, more recently, they had turned to roomier and more comfortable high-performance tourers.

Indeed, these newer Ferraris had their appeal. As Henry Manney noted in *Road & Track*, Ferrari had "a good racing name that gives vast publicity, there are parts and service in most civilized areas, and in recent years his cars have become quite fashionable to drive in spite of the stiff price tag."

So, all the *Cavaliere* had to do was beat the long-entrenched *Commendatore* at his own job—a formidable task. One thing Ferrari didn't wholly subscribe to was the "customer is king" philosophy of business, at least his non-racing business. Those willing to ride with the Sign of the Prancing Horse often had to put up with distinctly, well, cavalier treatment.

Despite their impressive performance and undeniable mechanical spirit, roadgoing Ferraris were seldom at the forefront of automotive design. Engines, chassis, suspensions, brakes, body engineering—none were really state-of-the-art. The reason for this was that roadgoing Ferraris existed mainly to generate revenues for supporting the factory's racing efforts. The imperious *Commendatore* considered his road-car buyers no more than a necessary evil and would take no more trouble over them than was necessary.

Two obvious lines of attack lay open to Lamborghini, one human, the other

mechanical. His open, straightforward, friendly nature almost guaranteed success with the first. As for the second, how better to please a keen, knowledgeable, discriminating enthusiast like himself than by building a car that he would like to own?

Ferruccio laid down definite guidelines for both the concept and layout of his ideal *gran turismo*. It would be a two-seater. However, the car would also be large and substantial so its wealthy owners could be comfortable and be able to accommodate a friend. It would be a closed coupe for quiet, refined, all-weather travel, and would naturally have every motoring luxury of the day. While it needn't be laden with technology, its specifications would be as advanced as Lamborghini's talented, experienced staff and large, ultramodern factory could achieve.

Oh yes, Ferruccio also specified that his GT must undercut Ferrari pricing by at least one million lire, then equivalent to about $1600.

The heart of any car is its engine, and Lamborghini knew that whatever else it might be, his car must have its own powerplant. A proprietary engine just wouldn't be in keeping with the image he wanted to establish, and there were few suitable choices anyway. Earlier, Giotto Bizzarrini had settled on Chevy power for his own models, as a practical decision; he had the ability to design an all-new super engine, but not

After several years of development, the 350 GT emerged in 1964. The car was an improvement in every way over the previous 350 GTV prototype. Wheelbase was increased 3.9 inches to 99.5 inches, and the car was finally given an engine. With 12 cylinders and 270 bhp, this engine would become a cornerstone at Lamborghini.

the resources to build it. Ferruccio's situation was far different, of course. With an entire industrial empire at his command, he most certainly had the wherewithal to produce his own engine.

That engine was bound to be a V-12. Not only because Ferrari had built his reputation with them and not just because of its advantages in smooth-

9

ness and flexibility, but for the prestige. Because Italy's motor-vehicle tax system put disproportionate levies on engines with more than four cylinders, only the wealthy could afford V-12s, so that's naturally what Ferruccio would produce.

Bizzarrini still had the drawings for a pure racing engine he'd designed while at Ferrari. It was a tiny jewel of a thing, having been intended for the 1.5-liter Grand Prix formula then in force. However, in basic architecture it was precisely what Lamborghini wanted for his forthcoming street car: a modern short-stroke, four-camshaft V-12 capable of ultra-high performance. Ferrari, of course, had long offered V-12s, in displacements ranging from 3.0-5.0 liters by that point. Yet their basic designs dated from the early 1950s and the street versions had only a single cam per cylinder bank.

As Bob Wallace recalls, Ferruccio proposed something like this to Giotto: "Draw me up a version of your four-cam race engine for street use, and make it as big as Ferrari's 3.0-liter if you can. How much money do you want?"

"I'll make it bigger," Bizzarrini replied, "And I'll also make it more powerful—a lot more powerful. In fact, you don't have to pay me until the first engine goes on the dyno and it makes more power than the Ferrari. Then you pay me X-amount of lire for every extra horsepower. Deal?" With that, Bizzarrini went to work.

This completely new engine had cylinders arrayed at the 60-degree angle that gives a natural dynamic balance to such engines (because of their 60-degree firing intervals). There were two valves per cylinder, each inclined at 35 degrees to the cylinder axis and fitted with double valve springs and inverted-bucket cam followers.

With bore and stroke of 77 × 62 millimeters (3.03 × 2.44 inches), total displacement was precisely 3464.5 cubic centimeters (211.4 cubic inches). The block was aluminum—cast, incidentally, by the small, struggling firm of ATS—with shrunk-in iron cylinder liners. Like other contemporary high-performance Italian powerplants, the liners were deliberately made long. This would allow them to stand proud of the gaskets for improved sealing when the heads, also of aluminum, were bolted down.

The crankshaft, beautifully machined from nickel-chromium billet steel, ran in seven main bearings, each held firmly by four bolts. Stout forged-steel connecting rods carried forged-aluminum pistons domed to give a compression ratio of 11.0:1 or better, according to Wallace. For quiet operation, the camshafts were driven not by gears but through a pair of chains, one for each cylinder bank. To avoid a narrow space between opposing camshafts, intake porting ran down into the centers of the heads, alongside the spark plugs. Exhaust porting was conventional. Dry weight of this potent power package was said to be 232 kilograms, or 512 pounds.

Lamborghini built only one 350 GTV prototype, and critics lashed out at its styling. The design of the rear end was especially criticized. Franco Scaglione rendered the original design, however Ferruccio had it altered to his tastes. Notable features on the show car that did not make it into production were the pop-up headlights and the sextet of exhaust pipes. Though this car carried no engine, a separate chassis and engine were developed for the car. It was this chassis that carried over into the 350 GT.

Lamborghini's engine would retain this basic architecture for many years, but a few features were seen mainly on this original version: dry-sump oiling system, a pair of conventional upright spin-on filters standing at the front of the engine, and dual Marelli distributors, one for each bank, sticking out from the intake cams at the rear. For the first V-12 a total of six twin-barrel, 36-mm Weber racing carburetors were mounted in downdraft position.

In unveiling the GTV, Lamborghini said that he'd considered fuel injection and had even experimented with various systems. Wallace, however, says this never went beyond the mockup stage, fuel injection being rejected due to its high cost and minimal benefit.

According to Lamborghini historian Rob de la Rive Box, the new V-12 first roared into life on May 15, 1963, on the company's Schenk dynamometer. It was a magic moment. Giuliano Pizzi was in charge. In a gentle first run-up to 4500 rpm he saw 226 horsepower on the European-standard DIN scale, about 235 bhp in today's SAE net measure. Sometime later he twisted it to 8000 revs and saw 360 DIN (374 SAE net). History records that as the official figure, although Wallace, as previously noted, says the ultimate numbers that determined Bizzarrini's payment were even higher.

No matter. The project was off to a good start. More castings were ordered from ATS and, with Bizzarrini out of the picture, Dallara was instructed to detune the V-12. His boss was happy with the demonstration of its potential. Yet for road use he wanted a smooth, quiet, tractable and unstressed engine good for 40,000 hard miles between services. The dyno began humming to that end, with Stanzani and Wallace working under Dallara's direction. One Lamborghini legend says they installed a development engine in one of Ferruccio's Ferraris for real-road testing, but Wallace debunks this as another bit of fanciful fabrication.

Mounted at the front of its chassis, the V-12 would drive through a Fichtel & Sachs clutch to an aluminum-cased ZF five-speed manual gearbox, both from Germany. Shocks were absorbed in the propeller shaft with a pair of rubber couplings rather than conventional U-joints. Behind that was a British-made Salisbury differential with limited-slip, the same final drive Jaguar used in its E-type.

That chassis was equally worthy of the superb engine. Suspension was independent at each corner via coil springs and tubular wishbones, and both ends enjoyed the ministrations of an anti-roll bar. British Girling disc

brakes with mild assist from a deliberately weak booster rode within 15-inch-diameter Borrani wire wheels. Tires were Pirelli Cinturato HS models, plump for the day at 205 mm wide and rated for a top speed of up to 160 mph. Steering, also by ZF, was a worm-type mechanism. However, the system had to have many jointed links to get around the bulky engine.

The Modena fabrication firm of Georgio Neri and Lucciano Bonacini welded up the GTV's steel chassis, which was a round-tube racing-type structure designed by Bizzarrini. The wheelbase was given as 2450 mm, or 95.6 in. Front and rear track measured 1380 mm/53.8 inches.

Cloaking these lovely components was a less-than-lovely body, though the styling seems to have reflected Ferruccio's tastes and his considerable input. In general, Lamborghini wanted a coupe with aggressive aerodynamic lines and plenty of glass. In particular, he asked for sleeker frontal styling á la Jaguar E-type and the tapering tail of an Aston Martin DB4.

As any commercial artist knows, a client with rigid insistence on his own ideas only makes a job tougher. Time was apparently very limited, too. These factors may explain some more unfortunate aspects of the GTV's styling. What puzzled many at the time was Ferruccio's choice of designer: Franco Scaglione, the former Bertone stylist whose previous high point had been the attention-getting, but bizarre, Alfa Romeo BAT show cars of the mid-Fifties.

The Lamborghini that emerged from his drawing board had similarly extreme flourishes and jutting angles, though the overall shape was essentially pleasing. What spoiled it was an unharmonious conglomeration of bold curves, sharp edges, odd proportions, and awkward details.

For example, there was a gaping "mouth" grille with a vertical divider bar that ran up the hood. It came off as a heavy-handed rendition of the "nostril" effect, and related to nothing else on the car. Also a little odd, if undeniably practical for outward vision, were the very tall rear window and generous rear quarter windows. The car's hidden headlamps, still a novelty in '63, were housed in a giant front-hinged hood/fenders structure something like the E-type's. A small but workable

trunk lay across the rear between twin fuel tanks, while six under-bumper exhaust pipes, three per side, called attention to the mighty V-12 up front. Like many show cars, the GTV was without windshield wipers. On the hood, to the left of the central rib, was the Lamborghini "charging bull" emblem already familiar in the tractor world.

The Turin GTV measured 175.5 inches long, 63.6 inches wide and 47.6 inches high. Its listed weight was 1050 kg/2314 pounds, but other sources put it at 980/2161. Any such figures—including published performance data—have to be theoretical projections, because the car was never finished. "It was a non-runner," says Bob Wallace. "The engine was never installed. The car was put on display at the show with a crate of ceramic tiles in the engine compartment."

The car's skin was a handmade mixture of steel and aluminum paneling by *Carrozzeria Sargiotto* of Turin, which Scaglione was operating. Obviously done in haste and built by workers more used to making molds for a plastics factory than automobile bodies, the 350 GTV drew criticism for its careless build and poor finish. Comments ran like "Ferruccio's Folly," and there was no shortage of predictions of financial ruin for the ambitious millionaire automaker.

Still, the bold, metallic-blue GTV attracted attention. The world was evidently starved for such a car, for press coverage was extensive. Ferruccio made the most of it, eagerly welcoming reporters to his impressive new factory and cheerfully revealing the various ideas his team was working on. One of them was apparently a competition version of the 350 GTV.

It's always been said that Ferruccio had an interest in racing but no interest in participating in it. There's hard evidence, though, that he was talking about a competition car based on his new roadgoing GT even at this early stage. Journalists who spoke with him reported as much. Griff Borgeson, for example, told readers in the February 1964 *Road & Track* that the original high-output engine and short-wheelbase design had "not been abandoned," but "moved to the back burner until the production-car program is far enough along to permit resurgence of Lamborghini's desire to go racing."

The Bizzarrini-designed engine (*top*) was used on the 350 GTV prototype. In final form it developed 360 bhp at 8000 rpm. On the production 350 GT the tall top-mount carburetors were replaced with sidedrafts to clear the car's low hoodline. The chassis of the 350 GTV was state-of-the-art. It sported an all-independent coil-spring wishbone suspension and Girling disc brakes. A Modena firm headed by Georgio Neri and Lucciano Bonacini welded up the racing-type round-tube frame. It was considerably stiffer than any of its competition.

Photos taken in the factory around that time often show two bare chassis. One, identified by Borgeson as a *corsaiola* or competition chassis, was made entirely of round tubing. Accompanying text referred to a race-tuned 3.5-liter V-12 with an estimated 350 bhp. Both car and engine were described as planned for production. The impression was that the source of the information was Ferruccio Lamborghini himself.

Chris Harvey, author of *The Lamborghinis*, had a different explanation. He said this lightweight tube frame was the first chassis built, and that it was designed by Bizzarrini at a stage when he hoped Lamborghini would go racing. "But when it became clear that the touring version had priority, Dallara had the frame reconstructed in heavier material." This makes sense, as two chassis were often seen in pictures.

Bob Wallace dismisses the *R&T* story. "Naw, that was just a proposal." He recalls that the round-tube display frame was simply the first mockup of the GTV chassis; a duplicate rested under the GTV show car. Any plans for a *corsaiola* model went no further than that. Indeed, beyond a trio of experimental vehicles that Wallace built in his spare time years later, there never was anything that can be described as a racing Lamborghini automobile. If Ferruccio did harbor a competition itch, as many of his employees did, he managed to curb it.

The GTV's specifications and theoretical performance may have been compelling. However, it became clear that the automotive establishment did not think much of its appearance, so the mockup quietly disappeared from view. Talk of its imminent production and eventual competition stopped. Ferruccio ordered that all work be directed toward the strictly roadgoing vehicle he'd envisioned from the beginning. Meanwhile, he began shopping around for someone to revise the styling.

History thus records the GTV as something of a failure, but that's an unkind appraisal. With the clarity of hindsight we can see this awkward prototype as merely a first step toward a goal that was ultimately and successfully realized. Moreover, it was quite an ambitious effort, and much about it was good. Given the great Lamborghinis to come, perhaps the only thing that was really wrong about the GTV was that Ferruccio let us see it.

Lamborghini was not deterred by the bad press and lukewarm public reaction to his GTV prototype. So the styling was a little off; that could be fixed easily enough. What mattered was that his vision of a Lamborghini *gran turismo* was no longer just a dream. He moved quickly, and within five months of the Turin auto show had in hand his first production car. It was a substantially new vehicle and was designated 350 GT, Ferruccio having apparently determined the *veloce* description unnecessary. The bull was about to charge.

The most obvious difference between the GTV and the 350 GT was the sheetmetal. One of Italy's most respected old-line coachbuilders landed the Lamborghini body contract. It was *Carrozzeria Touring* of Milan, responsible

The prototype's pop-up headlights were replaced with powerful Cibies on the production 350 GT (*top*) and a single windshield wiper appeared. Design work on this car was done by *Carrozzeria Touring* of Milan. The new design was much cleaner, especially at the rear and on the bodysides. The original GTV engine was completely redesigned with sidedraft carbs, a lowered compression ratio, and single oil filter (*right*). In addition, cam profiles were softened and platinum-tipped spark plugs were used. These revisions generated a very tractable engine that produced a highly competitive 270 bhp.

for the handsome Aston Martin DB4 and the similar Maserati 3500 GT, and many other styling successes over the years. Its designers began working their magic on Ferruccio's unfortunate GTV in late 1963.

Meanwhile, the Lamborghini development team carried out an extensive under-skin revision. Engineering chief Giampaolo Dallara had Neri & Bonacini make up a completely different chassis (seen as a display piece in many early factory photos). Instead of the previous network of round-section members, it had a basic "floor" of square and rectangular steel tubing, plus a couple of round-tube super-structures fore and aft to carry the suspension. Suspension was unchanged,

though the arms at both ends were now steel pressings instead of welded tubes.

Though quite a few sources maintain that the GT rode the GTV wheelbase, this is an error. For one thing, simply comparing profiles reveals that the GT has a much more open, expansive side window area and a less hunched roofline. More conclusive evidence is a Touring technical drawing

that calls out 2550 millimeters/99.5 inches between wheel centers, not 2450/95.6. (The same drawing, incidentally, indicates a length of 175.5 inches, the same as the GTV's published 175.5.) To clinch the matter, measuring a 350 GT shows that, sure enough, wheelbase is 99.5, 3.9 inches longer than the GTV's.

Touring's schematic also shows a 2-plus-1 configuration, with a third

Early 350 GT prototypes were fitted with a third seat, but that was replaced with a parcel shelf in production models. The Touring body was a hand-hammered mixture of steel and aluminum. The interior (*left*) was very comfortable for two people and featured a fully-instrumented dash. Before the production 350 was ready, the factory built several prototypes (*below*); note the full width front bumper and oil cooler mounted below the front spoiler. It is cars like this one that Bob Wallace drove across Italy, testing the suspension and various components for quality. Many of these cars were destroyed in crash testing in efforts to demonstrate that the cars could meet safety regulations.

Though the 350 GT retained the GTV's trunkback, most of the other design features were not carried over. Taillights were simplified, air scoops were dropped, and a back-up light was installed. Only 120 350 GTs were built between 1964 and '66, making it rare even by Lamborghini's standards. One exceptional feature of the early cars was the use of Borrani wire wheels.

bucket seat mounted behind the primary pair atop the driveline tunnel. At least one car with this layout (and small storage bins either side of the third seat) was photographed. Bob Wallace recalls that several early cars were built this way. However, he believes they were all later converted to the final production configuration, in which the cramped little third seat was replaced by a simple bench. This was mainly intended as auxiliary luggage space (its flat portion had two chrome scuff rails and the rear bulkhead was trimmed in leather). The space could accommodate very small passengers on very short trips.

As for the exterior, Touring saved the best of what Scaglione had wrought and simplified the rest. They removed the GTV's "prow," the vents behind its four wheel arches, and the full-length beltline trim above them. The six exhaust tips became four, and rear corners were rounded off to match the rest of the car. Wiping the windshield was a single large blade pivoted at the bottom center of the tall windscreen. The screen itself was raked at 65½ degrees from vertical according to the aforementioned Touring sketch.

So far so good, but what a pity that the GTV's unitized front sheetmetal and the generous engine access it provided were lost to a conventional hood. More disturbing was the decision to extend the headlights from the nose in the fashion of a "bugeye" Austin-Healey Sprite. All in all, this wasn't the most beautiful example of Italian automotive design, but Lamborghini's GT was elegant and distinctive.

Touring was also contracted to build the bodies, for which it naturally employed its famous, patented *Superleggera* ("super-light") construction. This type of body incorporated a framework of small steel tubes skinned with aluminum panels. Still, the 350 GT's official dry weight ended up at roughly 1050 kilograms or 2310 pounds. This was up from the higher numbers given for the GTV by a substantial 200 pounds.

Per Ferruccio's instructions, chief engineer Dallara detuned the Bizzarrini-designed V-12 and revised several details in the interest of a smoother, more pleasant, longer-lasting engine. The elaborate and costly racing-type dry-sump system was deemed unnecessary and gave way to a conventional oil pan. Because they raised engine position and because air cleaners had to be fitted, the expensive 36-mm vertical racing carbs were replaced by conventional sidedraft Webers, albeit with 40-mm bores. Compression was lowered from 11.0:1 to 9.5. Also, during the developmental stage, the exotic materials specified for the crankshaft and other components were cut back and cam profiles were softened.

Other changes to the original GTV engine included relocating the distributors to more accessible positions on the fronts of the exhaust camshafts, and adoption of a single, very tall Lamborghini-made oil filter. The production version also had expensive plat-inum-tipped spark plugs that could operate across a wider heat range and thus resist fouling in low-speed running.

After all this, the dyno showed "only" 270 DIN horsepower (280 bhp SAE net) at 6500 rpm. (As another example of the slippery nature of such figures, some Lamborghini information at the time quoted 280 bhp DIN.) Peak torque was listed as 239 pounds-feet at 4000 rpm.

Lamborghini's second shot at a "perfect" GT was shown to the world at the 1964 Geneva salon in March. This time the world liked what it saw and orders began coming in. However, initial demand was dampened by another of Italy's periodic financial crises, while supply was limited by the factory's decision to take things slowly. As Wallace has remarked, there were various teething troubles to sort out on both car and assembly line. So only 13 units went out through the end of the year, which suggests that Lamborghini was making every effort to realize his "perfect car." Indeed, a year-end audit showed he lost approximately $1000 on each of those 1964 cars.

No wonder. Engine machine work was exquisite (crankshafts came out "smooth as a baby's bottom," said an admiring Griff Borgeson) and mag-nafluxing was used liberally to ensure top quality. Every engine was first run by an electric motor for 10-12 hours, then under its own power for a like period. By installation it was fully power-checked and backed by a complete pedigree of dyno sheets. On completion, each car was turned over to Wallace for a thorough road test.

Ferruccio had done what he'd set out to do: craft a quiet, smooth, sophisticated high-performer that was technically ahead of anything Ferrari had been offering, yet easier to drive and generally faster, too. Ferrari's latest, the 275 GTB, also introduced in '64, was very aerodynamic and boasted all-independent suspension, but its V-12 still wasn't advanced as Lamborghini's.

Ferruccio had definitely outpointed Enzo's long-established 250 GT series. Those Ferraris had a 3.0-liter V-12, but with only one camshaft per cylinder bank, three carbs (versus Lamborghini's six), and about 240 claimed bhp in the typical roadgoing form. In addition, the Ferraris had only four speeds (except racers), a simple live rear axle, and mostly steel bodies instead of all-aluminum.

Ferrari also offered a 2+2 on the same 102.3-inch-wheelbase chassis as the 250 GT, but this was a different sort of car. In addition, he was still turning out very small numbers of his 4.0- and 5.0-liter Superamerica and Superfast two-seaters. With an alleged 400 bhp, they were obviously more potent than the new Lamborghini but also less sophisticated.

In all, Ferruccio had pulled a decisive coup. As for price, the 350 GT listed in the U.S. at $13,900 in 1965, just a bit less than Ferrari was charging for cars that weren't directly comparable.

Journalist and sometime Ferrari owner Henry Manney tested an early 350 GT for *Road & Track* in 1965 and had many positive things to say. On climbing in, he appreciated how the tall windshield merging into the roof created a light, airy feeling. He found the driving position "outstandingly

One interesting feature of the GT that was different from the prototype was the twin air inlets (*top*) on each side of the cowl. These were used not to cool the engine but to bring fresh air into the cockpit. The oddly shaped rear wheel wells were a carryover from the GTV, and together with the tight front wheel wells, gave the car a very low and aggressive look. Though the forward-opening hood offered good access to the 3465 cc engine, there was very little unused space. Note the especially complex mechanics of the throttle linkage (*right*) and two distributors in the 350 engine.

Variations on a Theme

Lamborghini was really rolling after the introduction of the 2+2, and Ferruccio began talking about a full four-seater. Touring used the 2+2 chassis as the basis for an avant-garde exercise that appeared at the annual Turin show in late '66. Named Flying Star II, after special bodywork the firm had done back in the 1930s, it was a small, sporty station wagon-style car.

Though it attracted attention, the Flying Star II was strictly a one-off and never a serious production prospect. Touring also did a convertible displayed at the Turin show. It was also, unfortunately, a swan song of sorts for the grand old Touring works, then in the serious financial trouble.

Luckily, Lamborghini owned the tooling for its two-seat and 2+2 bodies. In their last production year they were supplied by a spinoff firm composed of former Touring employees working under Mario Marazzi, who'd been in charge of Lamborghini body operations at Touring.

Another 2+2 chassis served as the basis for a one-off. On commission from an American customer, Neri & Bonacini, the shop that had built the original GTV chassis, did up a coupe (with a Ferrari windshield!) called Monza 400. It was a lean, rakish thing, much like a Le Mans or Mille Miglia racer of the previous decade, with lines both adept and awkward. It, too, led to nothing.

Zagato also did a one-off fastback called the 3500 GTZ, rakish and, for this *carrozzeria*, handsomely conventional. It was first seen at the 1965 Earl's Court motor show in London.

Neri & Bonacini did a one-off coupe (*above*), and Zagato tried its hand at a 350 GT revision (*top*). Though neither design amounted to anything, Lamborghini was always open to new design ideas and often built variations of the GT to meet customer needs.

box. (But noted that "the synchro pressure has been reduced from 20 lb. to five on the later gearbox.") Engine behavior was wonderful: flexible and smooth at the low end and strong at any rpm.

On an autostrada run with factory test driver Bob Wallace at the wheel, Manney looked over to see an indicated 174 mph (with Wallace muttering that the engine was 500 rpm down). *R&T*'s usual road-test data table showed the car geared for 152 mph at 7000 rpm, though Manney didn't claim it had reached that speed. Its final-drive ratio was 3.31:1, the taller (numerically lower) of two listed as available. Earlier reports, including original factory literature, quote a variety of other ratios. There's also a spread among reported top speeds. One that seems most likely has a 350 GT topping out at 149 mph (240 kph).

Whatever its true maximum, Manney was pleased to observe that "the Lamborghini seemed quite steady, even with a fair crosswind . . . I wouldn't hesitate to do it myself."

Wallace ran the obligatory acceleration runs in testing the car. It isn't clear whether *R&T* used his results or its own, but a 0-60-mph time of 6.8 seconds and the standing quarter-mile in 14.9 seconds at 93 mph were the numbers printed on the page. (One presumes these are "corrected," as the data table included *R&T*'s usual speedometer-error plot.) The magazine bought the quoted 2314-pound curb weight, which is frankly hard to believe. It got the wheelbase wrong, too, though the correct length was shown in an accompanying scale profile of the car.

During some twisty-road driving, the New Zealander who had described his as "the best job in the world" showed the American writer the value of the 350 GT's independent rear suspension. At the same time he provided an insight into the life of a factory road tester. "Bob gave me heart failure for a while until I saw what he was about," Manney wrote, "hopping hump-backed bridges to show that it landed straight, clapping on the binders from full noise to burn in the new pads, and even braking furiously in Ginther's Corner near Nonantola to show how stable the car was even with everything locked up. I must say that I was impressed, as the i.r.s. removed all

comfortable" despite pedals offset to the left and a seat that seemed low. He was impressed by the comprehensive instrumentation and overall finish that was "something you could be proud of."

On the road, Manney characterized the 350 GT as a "quickish, well-balanced car" with a "feeling of solidness." Admitting he was not one who quickly settled into a new car, he felt at home in the Lamborghini almost immediately. Its manual steering was especially well balanced: "Many high-performance cars require aiming rather than steering, but the Lamborghini's, in spite of strong self-centering action and not inconsiderable kickback from bumps at low speed, was extremely accurate." Manney judged the ride a bit stiff at low speeds and mentioned the heavy action of his car's early gear-

In 1966 Lamborghini introduced the 400 GT (*top*) to the public. Only 23 copies of this car were produced and three were skinned in lightweight aluminum. Only minor revisions were made to the interior of this model (*right*). Leather dash trim replaced polished aluminum in many areas. The major improvement was an engine that had increased to 3929 cc. The 400 GT had finally become the car Ferruccio wanted. *Road & Track* called the 400, "the finest GT car we've ever driven."

traces of hop or chatter while refusing to do any of the horrid things that i.r.s. is supposed to do. Likewise, he went teeming around the bends at full chat without a wiggle...."

"Purest joy," was Manney's verdict. "Driving a car like the Lamborghini is very good for the ego."

Other writers were similarly impressed. "Much less demanding to drive than a Ferrari," said *Car and Driver* in March of 1966, "so smooth, and so quiet." Yet in steering, braking, acceleration and handling, the 350 GT scored as well as the magazine's test Ferrari 275 GTS. That same month, *Sports Car Graphic* editors enthused about the Lamborghini's excellent ride on all surfaces, and said its combination of "roadability," lack of noise, good engine idle, and other assets made it "the most enjoyable 150-mph-plus car" they'd tried.

Despite such praise, Sant'Agata didn't rest on its laurels, continuously making little refinements and improvements to the 350 GT as production continued. Among these were revised grille styling, the addition of cowl air intakes, a second windshield wiper, a rear backup light, and substitution of leather dash trim for the early polished aluminum.

More important changes were made under the hood. The V-12 was enlarged to "four liters" via a bore stretch from 77 to 82 millimeters, bringing swept volume to 3929 cubic centimeters (239.8 cubic inches). That and a compression boost from 9.5 to 10.2:1 were said to add 50 horsepower for a new rating of 320 bhp DIN (332 SAE net), still at 6500 rpm. Torque improved, too, now 276 pounds-feet at 4500 rpm.

Also in 1966 Lamborghini introduced the 400 GT 2+2 (*right*). This car offered passable rear seat room for two additional passengers. In addition, the Cibie lights were replaced with four sealed beam units in an effort to meet certain government regulations. Many revisions were made to the original 350 GT body. The grill was altered (*top*), front fenders were of a different shape, and bumpers carried different curves. Inside, the front seating area remained much the same (*right*), but the roof was raised by 2.5 inches, creating more head room for rear seat passengers.

In this form the V-12 would establish the tone and image of Lamborghini cars for the next decade.

This engine was made optionally available in '65, resulting in a new 400 GT model. After testing one for its October 1966 issue, *Road & Track* termed it, "the finest GT car we've ever driven."

That assessment may seem a bit surprising, considering the 400 GT car was heavier and slower off the mark than the 350. Of course, there was reason. Experts generally agree that 143 original-type GTs were built between 1964 and '67. Just 23 had the 3.9 engine, and 20 of those were bodied not in "superlight" aluminum but in significantly heavier steel. Though *R&T* didn't mention it, its test 400 was obviously a steel-bodied car, as curb weight was listed as 3200 pounds. That sounds believable, and would account for the published 7.5-second 0-60-mph clocking and standing-quarter-mile time of 15.5 seconds at 92 mph. These numbers were noticeably inferior to those of the 350 GT tested the previous year, and came despite a shorter 4.08:1 final drive. *R&T* reported top speed as a marginally higher 156 mph.

Greater refinement was where the 3.9 engine scored over the 3.5. It was willing to run at any rpm, yet with a complete absence of fuss. It always started instantly and never oiled a plug, overheated, or did anything else uncivilized. Yet it produced the highest flat-out speed *R&T* had ever recorded for a road car. "It couldn't have been more impressive and we've never been more impressed." Then again, this was before the age of strangling emission controls.

The editors also praised interior equipment and finish as "excellent" and fully in keeping with the $14,250 price tag. Incidentally, the U.S.-market 400 had four circular sealed-beam headlights, and the test car displayed modest bumper over riders and two windshield wipers.

Dynamically, *R&T*'s testers were delighted with the 400's "remarkably light" steering, good handling, and stability, and the lack of both mechanical and aerodynamic noises. They did complain about heavy clutch and throttle action, and remarked that gearshift throws seemed rather long. But these were nits. "One drive and everyone had a new favorite car."

However, Ferruccio was not one to relax, and was already at work perfecting his car. Though the 400 GT was obviously an exceptional car, it lacked the utility of extra passenger and cargo room. In early 1966, Dallara was given the go-ahead to devote his time to converting the 350 GT into a genuine two-plus-two.

That car appeared at the ever-important Geneva salon in March 1966. You

Though the profile of the new 2+2 did not change much, close examination reveals differences. The doors (*below*) had a slightly different shape, and the rear side windows and backlight changed in shape as well (*below right*). Compared to the Countach in the background (*right*) the 400 GT looks pedestrian—but that was Ferruccio's point.

need a very close look to see it, but the 400 GT 2+2 bodies are really quite different from those of the 350/400 two-seaters. Primarily, they're about 2.5 inches taller, to fit the heads of rear passengers. They were also all were made of steel rather than aluminum, which meant they were heavier. However, your chances of seeing a 2+2 are greater. During its production years it outsold the two-seaters almost two-to-one.

Under the skin were more important changes that pleased the factory as much as customers. With the 400 GT 2+2, Lamborghini abandoned the German ZF transmission and British Salisbury differential in favor of units made completely in-house, a step that underlined Lamborghini's emergence as a full-fledged automaker, not just an assembler of components.

An interesting feature of the new transmission was that its Porsche-patent baulk-ring synchronizer system was used not only for all five forward gears but reverse as well. The shift pattern was conventional, with fifth up

The smaller rear window on the 2+2 (*below*) limited rearward visibility somewhat, but the car's stronger performance more than made up the deficit. All 2+2s were constructed with a steel body. This made the car more dent resistant but added weight. The new body design was a big hit with customers, and production soared to 224 units over the 2+2's brief two-year life.

and to the extreme right and reverse straight back from that. Lateral throws were rather wide, the mechanism noticeably spring-loaded so the lever would naturally stay in the middle (3-4) plane. Also, shift action was quite stiff, particularly when the gearbox oil was cold. The last made some wish for the old ZF, but everyone had to admit the new Lamborghini transmission was smoother and quieter. That was no accident. Each was put through a factory break-in regimen similar to that of every Lamborghini engine, with special pains taken to ensure quiet gear operation.

There have been some confusing reports over the years, but the 2+2 was built on the same 99.5-inch wheelbase as the two-seat 350/400. The small extra seats were just properly upholstered replacements for their baggage shelf. To make a little more room in that area, upper and lower rear suspension arms were reversed back to front. What had been linkage leading forward from the axle centerline now went aft. For more head room, Touring lowered the rear floorpan and raised the roofline by 2.5 inches. The 2+2 thus stood 50.1 inches tall instead of 47.6 inches.

Body panels were switched from aluminum to steel because the latter was easier to manufacture and more durable. The headlight system was changed to allow installation of U.S.-required circular sealed beams. Other departures from the two-seat models involved sharply reduced rear-window area (presumably so the Italian sun wouldn't bake back-seaters' heads so much) and a larger trunk and trunk lid. A single fuel tank of 23 U.S. gallons (87 liters) replaced the previous pair of 10.5-gallon tanks.

While it is true that the 2+2 was longer overall than the two-seaters, some

Ferruccio, true to his name, used a charging bull in the emblem on the hood of all GTs (*far left*). This would become his company's trademark. The engine of the 400 (*left*) was greatly revised over that of the 350. Bore was stretched from 77 to 82 mm and compression was bumped from 9.5 to 10.2:1. The new engine was rated at 320 bhp at 6500 rpm and offered 276 lbs/ft of torque at a low 4500 rpm. Because of the added weight of the steel body 0-60 mph times were lightly slower at 7.5 seconds, though top speed was up to 156 mph. The new engine was also more refined that the previous model and offered usable power at any rpm.

believe that the rake of its windshield and rear window were changed. Actual measurement shows that both the 350 and the 400 2+2 have the same 67.5-inch-wide wheelbases, but the body of the 2+2 is slightly longer at 180.9 inches. This is 5.4 inches longer than the 350 GT, partly due to bumper size. Windshields, moreover, have been proven by owners to be interchangeable.

Chassis elements were virtually untouched, save the aforementioned rear suspension. There, stiffer springs and shocks and revised wishbones were also decreed to handle a slight increase in weight. According to hard drivers familiar with the two-seater, these changes introduced a bit of tail-happiness into the 2+2's handling.

Of course, the 400 GT's 320-horsepower engine was retained. However, the higher roofline and resulting greater frontal area meant that the 2+2 was only about as fast all-out as a 350 GT. Yet apart from the Lamborghini transmission's stiffer shift action, the 2+2 was at least as pleasant to drive as a two-seat 400.

In all, the 400 GT 2+2 was one of Lamborghini's more successful models, with 247 sold. Incidentally, its U.S. list price was $14,750, about $500 upstream of the 400 GT. That represented a surcharge of $250 for each of those new rear passengers.

Some Lamborghini historians mention higher-performance versions of the 400 GT. One has described a mysterious vertical-carburetor engine displayed at the 1965 New York auto show, another says a '400 GTV' unit was optionally available. Bob Wallace, who ought to know, says it wasn't so: "If a customer wanted to pay for it, we

would fit things like polished connecting rods and maybe polish the ports a little. But all the engines were basically the same. There was never any such thing as a '400 GTV'. The only vertical-carburetor engine—except the Miura, of course—was that first dyno test engine. There only was the one of those, and it was a balls-out racer. It never went into a car. Aw, we did have a second one, but that was just a mock-up for display purposes."

Overall, many believe the 350/400 GT, with its smooth lines, light aluminum body and two-seat layout was the most appealing, most elegant car ever made by Lamborghini. It was the car Ferruccio Lamborghini had set out

to make, the closest to his original concept. It could thus be argued that some later models—the high-style, hyperenergetic ones with the names taken from bullfighting—were less "true" Lamborghinis than these first ones.

Think "Lamborghini" today and the vision is of rakish, ultra-high-performance mid-engine two-seaters. To Ferruccio, however—and to many aficionados of the marque—the quintessential Lamborghini was something quite different. He thought of it as a maturely stated four-seat coupe. More practical and less emotional than a Countach or Miura, this Lamborghini more accurately expresses Ferruccio's original automotive impulse.

model	1963 350 GTV	1964-66 350 GT	1965-66 400 GT	1966-68 400 GT 2+2
production	1	120	23	247
engine	dohc V-12	dohc V-12	dohc V-12	dohc V-12
displacement cc/ci	3465/211	3465/211	3929/240	3929/240
horsepower @ RPM (DIN)	360 @ 8000	270 @ 6500	320 @ 6500	320 @ 6500
torque @ RPM (lbs/ft)	240 @ 6000	239 @ 4000	276 @ 4500	276 @ 4500
length (mm/in.)	4500/175.5	4500/175.5	4500/175.5	4640/180.9
width (mm/in.)	1630/63.6	1730/67.5	1730/67.5	1725/67.3
height (mm/in.)	1220/47.6	1220/47.6	1220/47.6	1285/50.1
wheelbase (mm/in.)	2450/95.6	2550/99.5	2550/99.5	2550/99.5
track, front (mm/in.)	1380/53.8	1380/53.8	1380/53.8	1380/53.8
track, rear (mm/in.)	1380/53.8	1380/53.8	1380/53.8	1380/53.8
weight (kg/lbs)[1]	1050/2314	1050/2314	1380/3042	1380/3042

[1]Factory dry-weight claims, actual numbers higher.

CHAPTER TWO

ISLERO

INTRODUCED AT THE WRONG
MOMENT, THE ISLERO HAD TO
SHARE THE SPOTLIGHT WITH THE
FUTURISTIC ESPADA. THOUGH IT
ALWAYS REMAINED IN THE
SHADOWS, THE ISLERO WAS
SUPERIOR TO ITS PREDECESSORS
AND ITS COMPETITION.

Lamborghini's Islero, a reskin of the 400 GT 2+2, was doomed from the start. At the Geneva auto show in 1966, the Miura was introduced and changed the history of Lamborghini and the cars it would produce. Then at the '69 Geneva salon, the Islero had to share the limelight with the futuristic Espada. It was a car that, for all the world, appeared to be a warmed-over version of the 2+2, so it's a wonder the Islero survived at all.

Yet the Islero was more than just the last Lamborghini built off the original GTV chassis, it was the fulfillment of Ferruccio's dream to build a luxury GT car. He had more direct influence on this car than any except the original GTV. This was the last Lamborghini that was truly from the mold that Ferruccio had created for the marque.

It helps to understand that men of maturity and wealth were supporting a healthy little market for true GTs with additional, "occasional" seats. These buyers insisted upon mechanical excellence. The Islero delivered on that account with an aluminum, quad-cam V-12 and all-wheel independent suspension with disc brakes. The interior included comprehensive gauges and controls, luxury appointments, and more room for rear seat passengers.

These customers were men of business and industry and finance, not *lotharios*, and so their car's shape had to be refined, seasoned. The lines of the Islero were most certainly restrained.

In fact, Ferruccio had a strong hand in its styling. The Islero was so much a reflection of *Il Cavaliere's* taste that whenever he wanted to go somewhere in one of his cars at the time, this is the one he generally chose.

Mario Marazzi and his group of ex-Touring employees were now building the bodies for the 400 GT and 400 2+2. But the basic 350/400 shape was now approaching five years of age, and it became obvious a reskin was necessary. So, Ferriccio enlisted the help of Marazzi and the two of them went to work on a successor.

Riding the original 350/400 square-tube chassis, the Islero employed steel body panels attached to the 400 2+2's inner structure. Wheelbase remained at 99.5 inches, but track dimensions were widened a bit as Lamborghini took advantage of developments in tire science. Because the rubber was better, Bob Wallace had to revise the suspension with stiffer anti-roll bars front and rear. Though the prototype appeared on Borrani wire wheels, production Isleros rolled on spiffy cast Campagnolos like those of the Miura and Espada.

It is probably good that the Espada stole much of the Islero's thunder at the '68 Geneva show. When the Islero made its debut, it was poorly finished—not unlike the original GTV. For reasons that must have seemed sound at the time, Ferruccio repeated the fundamental error he'd made with his very first car. Thus, not only was

the new Marazzi body not that pretty, it wasn't that well finished, the interior in particular.

"That was everyone's fault and no one's fault," says Wallace of this situation. "Marazzi was just a bunch of ex-Touring people and they just didn't have the resources. There was never enough money or equipment available to do the job properly."

Still, the Islero's many good points overshadowed this bad one. Though no limo, it was roomier than the 400 2+2, especially in back, and glass area was more generous. That glass, by the way, was bent in only one dimension as a cost-cutting move (the previous Touring-design windows had all been compound-curve). Soundproofing was also increased.

Overall, the Islero was 4.5 inches shorter than the last 400 GT 2+2 and, although Lamborghini weights are always debatable, was believed to be considerably lighter. The notably high-set bumpers at both ends were an obvious benefit. But most important, the Islero had all the strong, silent performance of the original GTs that had made the world take note of Lamborghini. It also had the marvelous, Bizzarrini-designed V-12 that was as content to trickle along in traffic as it was willing to rocket down the road.

After building 125 Isleros—and taking criticism of their problems to heart—Lamborghini began turning out a significantly improved model in late

Though based on the same chassis as the 350/400 GT, the Islero was basically a new car. Up front, the exposed headlights were gone (*above*) and rounded curves gave way to angular lines. In addition to new glass and sharp lines at the rear (*right*), the suspension was revised to take advantage of new tire technology. The track was also enlarged and the engine updated to develop more horsepower. While many disliked the new styling, Ferruccio is said to have liked this car best, and often used it as his daily driver.

summer 1969. This Islero S, or GTS as some literature called it, had a mildly reworked exterior, a completely redesigned interior, several suspension improvements, and a much more potent engine.

Most noticeable among the body alterations were a "mailbox slot" air exhaust vent behind each front wheel, and a slight flare to all wheel arches. Also, fixed triangular panes were added on the front portion of each door window (previously one-piece). Closer inspection revealed a more prominent hood air intake and small inlets in front, flanking the main radiator opening. Fog lights hanging beneath the front bumper were standard, as were all-around tinted glass and an electrically heated rear window.

Inside, the Islero driver found improved seating, with higher front backrests and split rear seatbacks flanking a fold-down armrest. The original, somewhat haphazard, gauge layout was more orderly, and safer non-protruding rocker switches replaced push-pull knobs. In place of the dash-mounted passenger grab bar was a proper glovebox, which had been missing before.

Rear suspension was revised in detail, with Espada-like components

Inside the original Islero (*left*), toggle switches and push-pull knobs were carry-overs from the 400 GT 2+2. These would be replaced on the improved Islero S model, but the dash layout would remain the same. Also on the S, the rear seats were divided by a center console and a glovebox replaced the passenger grab handle. Many original Isleros were later modified to S specifications (*above*). Behind the front wheels on the S version was a horizontal mail-slot-like vent, though this car was modified with a vertical vent. The Islero S also had subtle wheel well flares to accommodate larger tires.

that improved stability under hard braking and acceleration. The changes were useful, as the brakes were larger and more powerful and the V-12 was pumped up with the 10.8:1 compression and hotter cams from the Miura S. That gave a claimed 350 horsepower at 7500 rpm and a top speed of 161 mph, according to contemporary road tests. The Islero S was a real businessman's express.

All these improvements came a bit late. Time and reputation had turned most people against the car. Also, because of all the media attention being paid to the Miura and Espada, there was little allowance left for the revised Islero.

One of the rare road tests that gives us a feel for the S appeared in Australia's *Sports Car World* magazine in May 1970. A sign that early quality problems had been solved was Graeme Harris's finding that the Islero now had "no mistakes" and embodied "perfection of workmanship." He also appreciated that it was short enough to park easily yet offered ample front leg room. The low 4¼-inch ground clearance was a worry, and it's obvious from photos how items like mufflers, the front-mounted oil cooler, and the rear anti-roll bar hung too close to the road.

Sports Car World found the Islero capable of 0-60 mph in 6.2 seconds and

160 mph at 6500 rpm all-out, yet "well tamed for city driving." Both clutch and throttle seemed heavy, but the power-assisted brakes were quite light. In all, Harris decided that "motoring in the Islero is ecstatically safe, with untouched power in hand to pull the car through any approaching danger...."

Had it been the only Lamborghini of its time, the Islero might have been viewed more favorably, then and now. But it lacked curbside presence next to the almighty Miura and exotic Espada. The car's $20,000 sticker price was another drawback. The last Islero left Sant'Agata on April 15, 1970.

With just 225 built, including a mere 100 S-models, the Islero cannot be described as an overwhelming success. Yet, in many ways the S model was arguably the best of the front-engine Lamborghini GTs. It was most certainly the closest Ferruccio ever came to building his dream car, and that makes it the kind of success anyone with automotive soul will value.

model	1968 Islero	1969 Islero S
production	125	100
engine	dohc V-12	dohc V-12
displacement cc/ci	3929/240	3929/240
horsepower @ RPM (DIN)	325 @ 7000	350 @ 7500
torque @ RPM (lbs/ft)	289 @ 5500	289 @ 5500
length (mm/in.)	4525/176.5	4525/176.5
width (mm/in.)	1730/67.5	1730/67.5
height (mm/in.)	1300/50.7	1300/50.7
wheelbase (mm/in.)	2550/99.5	2550/99.5
track, front (mm/in.)	1380/53.8	1380/53.8
track, rear (mm/in.)	1380/53.8	1380/53.8
weight (kg/lbs)[1]	1315/2893	1315/2893

[1]Factory dry-weight claims, actual numbers higher.

The Islero engine (*above*) did not differ in displacement from the 400 GT 2+2, but horsepower was up from 320 to 350 bhp at 7500 rpm. This was accomplished with a higher compression ratio and hotter cams. At the rear of the Islero (*top*), there was more room than the 2+2 and glass was now bent in only one direction as a cost-cutting move.

CHAPTER THREE

ESPADA

LAMBORGHINI'S FIRST FULL

FOUR-SEATER, THE ESPADA,

STOLE THE SHOW AT ITS 1968

DEBUT IN GENEVA. AT THE TIME,

NO OTHER CAR LOOKED OR ACTED

LIKE IT. ITS FUTURISTIC DESIGN

AND SOLID CHASSIS ENABLED

THE CAR TO STAY IN PRODUCTION

FOR A FULL TEN YEARS.

Four-seat luxury-sports cars may be the trend today, but back in the late 1960s the focus of the automotive world was two-seat ultra-performance cars. Ferruccio Lamborghini had an advanced vision: He wanted to build the best four-seat luxury-sports sedan the world had ever seen. Many automakers had tried this before; Ferruccio was different because he succeeded.

His exotic Espada showed the others it could be done. When this car burst upon the scene in 1968, nothing on the road could rival its medley of four-place comfort, sports-car moves, and exotic-car looks. Few cars have matched it since. In production a full decade, it remains one of the most admired and commercially successful Lamborghinis. It was also among the few that should have survived longer than its ten-year lifetime. Even so, the Espada was the one car to live on after Ferruccio's departure from the company that fully embodied his own tastes.

The Espada's roots stand in a pair of 1967 Bertone show cars. One was the oddly named Marzal, which was an attempt to meet Ferruccio's desire for a genuine four-seater in the lineup. The other was just an oddity: a rebodied Jaguar E-type commissioned by a British newspaper. Both appeared when the front-engine 400 GT 2+2 was in production and the amazing mid-engine Miura two-seater was making

its mark. Given these models, there were big questions about a new Lamborghini: What would it look like, and where would its engine be?

One could easily imagine the Miura as the basis for a full four-seater, and the Marzal was built on this idea. Adding 4.5 inches to the Miura's 97.5-inch wheelbase—all ahead of its compact, transverse-midships V-12 power package—made room for the second set of seats. But in working out the details, chief engineer Giampaolo Dallara decided that the V-12 was too big and split it right down the middle to form a twincam slant-six of 1965 cubic centimeters. At the same time, Bertone's Marcello Gandini drew up a radical body with a huge gullwing door on each side that was virtually all glass. The marriage of this body and engine, built in 1966 and displayed at the annual Geneva salon early the next year, was undeniably striking. But it just wasn't what Ferruccio wanted.

Gandini's Pirana was more like it. Financed by London's *Daily Telegraph* as a publicity vehicle for a new weekend magazine, this daring and dramatic restyle of Jaguar's sports car premiered at the October 1967 London Motor Show. Though few people felt that the two-seat E-type needed restyling, the longer, 2+2 model was perhaps another matter. This 2+2 was the Pirana's basis.

In English that groped a little, a Bertone press release explained the thinking behind the Pirana design: "The car should have represented the ideal means for a certain type of man: high social level, love for sport driving, but no more spartan driving. A desire, then, to provide the car with all those technical contrivances granting to the passengers [sic] the best comfort, safety, relax and pleasure in driving." Sporty but not spartan: Wasn't that precisely what Ferruccio had been talking about?

The Pirana's actual wooden body buck was used to shape Bertone's second stab at a four-seat Lamborghini, the prototype for what ultimately became the Espada. It retained the Marzal's general shape, gullwing doors (albeit less glassy ones), and four seats, but put the engine up front. There was still some discussion about motive force. Ferruccio had an itch to offer a smaller, less exotic engine—like Dallara's slant-six, for instance. However, Dallara himself was proposing a V-12 enlarged to 4.5 liters. But there was no time for either, so the familiar 3.9-liter was pushed into service.

Moving the engine to the front provided more luggage room at the back of Gandini's egg-like body design. That would certainly be more desirable than the cramped space that would have been available in a mid-engine

Penned by Bertone's young styling chief, Marcello Gandini, and placed on a lengthened Miura chassis, the Marzal (*left*) was the predecessor of the Espada. It was a car so futuristic that even Ferruccio himself sent it back for revisions. Massive gull-wing doors filled with glass allowed easy entry into a surprisingly roomy interior (*below*). However, one concession to space had to be made, and Marzal had to make due with but half of the fabulous Miura V-12. The 2620 cc engine was rated at 175 bhp and sat behind the rear seats in the fully operational car. Dash layout (*below left*) reflected Gandini's hexagonal phase and Bertone's penchant for futuristic designs.

layout. The V-12 would sit "north-south" as in the 350/400 GTs, not sideways as in the Miura. But it would be set 7.9 inches further forward than the 350/400 to open up more cabin space. The old separate tube frame would be abandoned for what amounted to a semi-monocoque of sheet steel, as on the Miura. Tubular structures at each end would carry an improved version of the now-familiar all-independent Lamborghini suspension.

Though this attempt was still a bit ungainly, its essential lines were right. Further refinements (including replacement of the gullwings with conventional doors) were made for the final production prototype. This car was painted a spectacular metallic gold. Dubbed Espada, it went on show at Geneva in the spring of 1968 alongside the new Islero and S-version Miura—and promptly caused a sensation. Lamborghini had scored another coup, one almost as great as the original Miura two years earlier.

The Espada was a compelling blend of contrasts. It wasn't exactly beautiful to some eyes, but its daring distinctiveness certainly captured every eye. A sedan on the inside, it was a low-slung sports car outside. It gave the illusion of being large, but actually wasn't. Its 103.4-inch wheelbase, for example, was 3.9 inches longer than the 2+2 Islero's, but four inches shorter than that of the typical late-'60s American ponycar. Drivers discovered that the Espada felt like a small car when in motion, while two adults found adequate room in its sumptuous aft cabin. Ten cubic feet of luggage would fit under its racy, near-flat rear hatch without blocking vision. Its engine was masterful at both ends of the speed spectrum. Though ever so docile in traffic, this "family sports car" was not only the fastest four-seater on the market but also one of the fastest automobiles in the world.

Dimensions gave the Espada much of its visual impact. At 184.8 inches stem-to-stern it was about as long as a contemporary U.S. compact but broader of beam than most cars of the day, 72.5 inches wide. Height was perhaps most striking of all: a squat 46.2 inches, making the Espada 4.5 inches lower than the new Islero.

Nevertheless, a wheelbase 1.4 inches longer than the Marzal's allowed doors of sufficient length to grant passengers the same ease of entry that had been Gandini's intent with the Marzal gull-wings. As in the Miura, left- and right-side seats were well separated, here by a full-length center console that served as a route for ventilation ducts to the rear and increased chassis beam strength as well. Air ducts surrounding the engine bay were designed to add stiffness in that area. A 24.6-gallon fuel supply was carried by twin tanks, one on each rear fender (fillers were hidden inside little grilles there), thus lowering the luggage floor.

A number of reports credited the Espada with having aluminum body

After a year and a half of development, the Espada emerged from the Marzal's shadow. The new car (*right*) was the fastest production four-seater of its time. With a displacement of 3929 cc, the engine made 325 bhp at 6500 rpm, the same as the original Islero, but dual distributors were replaced with a single unit. Inside, the dash put everything within the driver's reach (*below*).

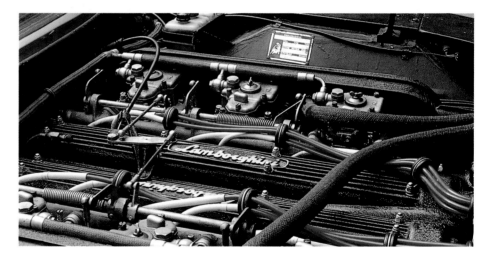

panels (some even warned they could be dented with a thumbnail), thus its fairly low curb weight. However, this was not so. The Espada's only aluminum panel was its hood; the rest was steel. It had to be, in order to weld to the steel floorpan. (Writers in rust-belt areas seem to avoid this mistake; one Englishman remarked that his test car showed signs of rust by the 10,000-mile mark.) Besides, the factory's quoted dry weight was 3575 pounds, a reasonably accurate figure for once.

Though rack-and-pinion steering was intended for the Espada, a ZF worm-gear mechanism with no power assistance was substituted. Suspension was like the Islero's except for improved geometry and softer spring, shock, and anti-roll bar rates. Brakes were discs at all four corners. Top speed was said to be a rousing 155 mph—again, close to reality.

Several Espada details were, in the vernacular of the day, as far out as its overall styling. Atop a notably low, flat hood were a pair of bold NACA-pattern air ducts that fed not the carbs, as some thought, but an elaborate cabin ventilation system. Engine-compartment air exited the front fenders via a pair of "mail slots" flanking each front-wheel arch, a developed version of an idea that had appeared on the gull-wing prototype (and would resurface on the Islero S). Rear side windows were hinged to swing out from the top. The nearly horizontal roofline and mostly glass rear hatch were worthy of frequent comment in 1968. As the resulting profile was better for aerodynamics than visibility, Bertone added a distinctive secondary vertical rear window below the hatch opening and above the taillights. (This feature was revived for the Bertone-styled Maserati Khamsin of 1974, and more recently was employed by Honda on its second-generation CRX.) The "hexagon-itis" that had afflicted Gandini on the Marzal flared up again on

the Espada instrument panel, though the symptoms were far less severe.

With bodywork mounted by Bertone at Grugliasco near Turin, what the factory called the 400 GT Espada began coming out of Sant'Agata Bolognese in the summer of '68. It would continue to do so into 1978—the longest production run for any Lamborghini to date save the Countach.

Those ten years produced three distinct Espada "series." What is now known as the "Series 1" was the group of cars built through 1969. During that brief period, a number of running changes were made. For example, a subtle but significant floorpan alteration increased rear headroom by 20 millimeters (about ¾ inch), the original opening front quarter-vents were

Early versions of the Espada rode on the same magnesium wheels as the Islero, Miura, and Jarama. The car's clamshell hood (*left*) offered generous engine access, and the NACA ducts fed the climate control system. The rear seating area was almost as luxurious as the front and offered true room for rear-seat occupants.

something similar, and Lamborghini evidently felt compelled to compete. But Lancomatic never found favor and quietly disappeared.

Bob Wallace explains why: "The idea was exceptionally good, but unfortunately it was a little ahead of its time. The technology available was such that they couldn't solve heat and friction problems with the seals, and the ride frequency was too harsh."

Another luxury touch was also floated for the Espada. According to marque historian Jean-Francois Marchet, "Ferruccio Lamborghini, a self-confessed woman's man, had even asked for servo assistance on the clutch...."But this was something he didn't get.

An early-1970 Brussels show was the stage for unveiling a "Series 2" model. It was called the "400 GTE Espada." Though its most visible alteration was an all-new instrument panel, rear passengers benefitted from additional ventilation and a new illuminated center armrest.

Technical improvements were more extensive: vented brakes all-around (replacing solid rotors), Lobro CV joints for the rear halfshafts, and newly optional power steering. The big event was the adoption of the high-compression Islero/Miura "S" engine (*sans* identifying letter) with 350 bhp at 7500 rpm on a 10.7:1 squeeze (previously 325 bhp @ 6500 rpm and 9.8:1). A later running change brought five-bolt wheels to replace the Miura-style center-locks originally used.

Under normal circumstances, the Espada would have been ready for

fixed, and grillework on the rear lower window was deleted. Unlike the haughty Enzo Ferrari, *Il Cavaliere* was always open to granting special customer favors, so one early Espada was built with a large fixed glass roof panel. At least one other example, a Bertone show project called V.I.P., was equipped with a TV and rudimentary dry bar in the rear seat.

More meaningful experiments in this period included something called "Lancomatic" suspension, unveiled at Turin '68. A hydropneumatic rear self-leveling system, it was developed in cooperation with its German manufacturer, Langen, a subsidiary of the large Ehrenreich suspension-component company. Ferrari's lush 365 GT 2+2 had arrived the previous year with

In 1973 Lamborghini introduced an updated version of the Espada. This model offered a revised interior (*above left*) and, believe it or not, a Chrysler three-speed automatic transmission. The car's radio was located to the left of the driver. Vents on either side of the front wheels exhausted hot air from the engine compartment. The engine itself offered 25 more horsepower, up to 350.

retirement by 1973. But Lamborghini's circumstances weren't exactly normal at that point, not least because of growing labor and economic troubles. Besides, Bertone and Lamborghini couldn't come up with anything better, so they decided to simply improve the Espada once more.

The result, introduced at the 1973 Turin show, was the retrospectively named "Series 3," identifiable by a mildly restyled nose and taillamps. Power steering (an improved ZF system) and air conditioning were newly standard, spring and shock rates rejiggered, rear suspension arms slightly altered, and brakes made more powerful. The dash was revised yet again, newly wrapped around toward the driver from the middle and matched by a more upright kickup from the front of the center console. Options were expanded to include a sunroof and, beginning in March '74, automatic transmission.

That latter item may seem curious for a thoroughbred Italian GT, but some customers with more money than driving ability apparently wanted one. To avoid the expense and bother of making its own, Lamborghini adopted Chrysler's excellent three-speed TorqueFlite (already familiar to Europeans in recent Chrysler-powered Bristols and the Jensen Interceptor from Britain), tightening a few tolerances but not altering its basic design. Unfortunately, full-throttle upshifts were set at 4800 rpm—fine for typical Detroit iron but not the Lamborghini V-12. With the automatic, the V-12 couldn't turn within 700 rpm of its torque peak, let alone reach the meati-

est part of its power band some 2000 rpm above.

Because of high demand in Europe only a very few Espadas went to American customers each year. Lamborghini hoped to sell more, but U.S. regulations insisted that all cars be desmogged. Accordingly, the factory devised a smog pump that cut out at high revs, leaving peak power unaffected; special carburetors and ignition settings completed the engine cleanup. The U.S. also required five-mph "impact" bumpers, so Sant'Agata drew up "safety" bumpers for the Espada. Though not as dreadful as some of that era, they hardly enhanced Gandini's lines.

Historian Rob de la Rive Box tallies a total of 1217 Espadas built in the decade-long production run, making this the most "common" Lamborghini except for the Countach.

It was the largest Lamborghini. But, the American magazine *Road Test* made the valid point that the low-slung Espada looked longer than it was. Still, even in lands with wide-open spaces, you knew you were "covering a lot of square feet on the road surface," according to Australia's *Sports Car World*. Ray Hutton, who drove an Espada from Sant'Agata to the *Autocar* offices in crowded London, found it "too big a car to throw around on narrow mountain roads." But fellow countryman Simon Taylor, reporting on a weekend of *Autosport* business in southern England, said it was "very maneuverable and seems to shrink around the driver as he gets used to it." With that, Taylor found that "the Espada could be booted through

roundabouts and tight corners like a car of half its size, weight and power."

Motor Sport's Denis Jenkinson found the suspension equally impressive. He explained you could feel the wheels undulating with surface changes, but the motions were well damped, the ride comfortable. "Comfort is easy to obtain," he wrote, "but directional stability coupled to good cornering, minimum roll or pitch and effectiveness at all speeds is another matter, and the Espada has all these and more."

Echoing this view was Australian Mel Nichols, a well-known Lamborghini admirer: "Offering handling, roadholding and stability that gives the car a natural cruising speed of 115 mph, it also offers one of the most supple rides in existence," he said in *Wheels*. "Many a limousine could learn a commendable lesson from it."

Conversely, the rear brakes tended to lock up early *sans* passengers and luggage. *Road & Track* thought Lamborghini should adopt some sort of automatic load leveling system, as Ferrari had for its 365 GT 2+2. Lamborghini was working on it, as noted, however it was never produced.

On the subject of brakes locking, detailed study of this literature reveals

model	1968-78 Espada
production	1217
engine	dohc V-12
displacement cc/ci	3929/240
horsepower @ RPM (DIN)	350 @ 7500[1]
torque @ RPM (lbs/ft)	280 @ 5500
length (mm/in.)	4738/184.8
width (mm/in.)	1860/72.5
height (mm/in.)	1185/46.2
wheelbase (mm/in.)	2650/103.4
track, front (mm/in.)	1490/58.1
track, rear (mm/in.)	1490/58.1
weight (kg/lbs)[2]	1625/3575

[1]325 bhp @ 6500 rpm on Series 1 models.
[2]Factory dry-weight claims, actual numbers higher.

Knock-off wheels were replaced with a slicker 5-bolt design on the second version of the Espada (*top*). Though rumors had the entire bodyshell being constructed of aluminum, only the hood received this special treatment. The rest of the panels were steel and welded to the car's frame. An interesting feature at the rear of the car was a second, fixed pane of glass (*above*), allowing the driver greater rearward vision.

a variety of observations. Some testers agreed with *R&T*, others reported front brakes locking first, and at least one found the brakes so perfectly balanced that they didn't lock at all. Such differences evidently reflect the different vehicles tested.

Similar discrepancies crop up about steering effort, but this was probably more a matter of differences in personal taste. Reporting on the early non-power-assisted Espada, some drivers spoke of how much muscle it took to steer. Others enthused about how light it felt.

What most everyone agreed on was the handling: superb. We let the experienced and eloquent Mr. Nichols speak for all: "Left to itself (that is, with a light or trailing throttle) the Espada is an understeerer. Coming through long bends, the front end wants to run out in a very wide line, away from the apex. This can be disconcerting and rather disappointing until you learn to squeeze on more throttle (the pedal, incidentally, has an extraordinarily long travel, but is sponge-soft), progressively increasing power as the car goes through the bend. The response is immediate—the car just runs around neutrally."

Despite its positive reception, by 1978 production of the car had ceased for several reasons. Sales had begun to tail off and the Espada was hardly the fresh face it had been a decade earlier, but the main reason was adverse circumstances affecting Lamborghini as a whole rather than any real deficiencies in the product. Remember that 1978 was the year the Italian courts took control of the company. Lamborghini's financial health had deteriorated to the point that suppliers demanded cash-on-delivery. Its body builder, Bertone, was its major supplier and its major creditor and, as Marchet records, "relations between Bertone and Lamborghini were at their coldest point." As the money-spinning Countach could be made completely in-house, it just didn't seem worth the struggle to keep the Espada going.

As with the Miura five years before, time had run out for one of the most interesting and appealing cars ever offered by an outfit renowned for interesting and appealing cars. The Espada would hardly be forgotten.

CHAPTER FOUR

JARAMA

WHEN COMPARED TO THE MIURA

AND ESPADA, IT WAS CLEAR THAT

THE ISLERO NEEDED TO BE

REPLACED. WHAT LAMBORGHINI

UNVEILED AT THE 1970 GENEVA

SALON WAS AN ENTIRELY

NEW CAR—THE JARAMA.

Though the Islero was a fine update of the aging 350/400 GT chassis, it had become clear by late 1969 that the car needed a fresh replacement. Up against the others in the Lamborghini stable, the sleek Espada supersedan and the sultry Miura sports car, the Islero could at best be considered quaint. In fact, the Islero's separate 350-era chassis was now low-tech at Lamborghini. So, after just two years, it was clear that a replacement was in order. It was called Jarama.

Urged by technical director and plant manager Paolo Stanzani, Ferruccio Lamborghini decided to hand over styling to Marcello Gandini at Bertone. Bertone would also press the body panels for the new car at its Grugliasco facility, and Marazzi would continue to assemble the shells.

This arrangement was economically and aesthetically sensible because the Islero's successor would ride a shortened version of the Espada chassis that Bertone was already making. Both ends of this sheet-steel platform, including drivetrain and suspension mounts, were left untouched. But 10.6 inches was pared from the middle, giving the new 2+2 the shortest wheelbase in Lamborghini history. At 92.8 inches it was 6.7 inches down on the Islero's and 2.8 inches shorter than that of the 350 GTV.

Being the shortest Lamborghini ever, one would expect the Jarama to be the lightest, but this was not the case. Actually, it was one of the heavi-

est. The reason for the excess weight was that the tiny Marazzi firm didn't have facilities anywhere near as specialized as Bertone's. According to Bob Wallace, this meant that the structure had to be built in layers, one panel over another. This inefficient construction partly explains why the Jarama ended "a good 600 pounds overweight," as Wallace growls now. Also, compared with previous Lamborghinis, the Jarama carried more of its total weight on the front wheels, as the engine was planted squarely between them. Shifting the battery to the trunk didn't do much to counterbalance that.

On the outside, the Jarama looked so different from both the Espada and the Miura that it's hard to believe Marcello Gandini had a hand in it. His design was different, but one that worked within a constraint. Like the Islero, the Jarama was the "businessman's Lamborghini," the sensible, deliberately unspectacular one—the one for people like the boss. Because the car was compared to the Miura and Espada, its body design was thought to be unimaginative. This was, however, an unjust theory, for the car was from a different mold and for a different purpose.

So Gandini drew an envelope that managed to harmonize a wide "bullet" nose with a boxy tail and trapezoidal side-window openings. The result was a roomy, glassy coupe with suppressed excitement in its sharp creases and muscular wheels. The car came across looking like a taut GT—at once practi-

cal and powerful, though perhaps more bold than beautiful. Its most distinctive styling feature was the headlamp treatment: fixed round quads semi-concealed via body-colored covers that pivoted down, like a snake's eyelids, when the lights were switched on.

The Jarama's name might have evolved from one of two sources. One source might have been the district in Spain that breeds fighting bulls. The second is the like-named racetrack outside Madrid that often entertained the Spanish Grand Prix in the late 1960s. Regardless, this new businessman's coupe was first seen at the Geneva motor show in the spring of 1970.

Reaction was decidedly mixed. Contemporary reports say some folks appreciated the audaciously innovative styling. Others, in the word of Italian writer Stefano Pasini, found it "disturbing." Most everyone, he went on, was bothered by the "mediocre" interior finish, "incomprehensible" controls, and "irrational" driver's seat. These "and other defects combined to give a rather negative picture of the Jarama."

Then there was all that weight. Though not a heavyweight, the Jarama was most certainly a cruiserweight. At 3388 lbs. it was almost 500 pounds heavier than the Islero and nearly as weighty as the Espada. Still, the Lamborghini V-12 was as magnificent as ever, and there were wider and stickier new Michelin tires, so the Jarama's

The Jarama (*left*) was based on a shortened Espada chassis, and many expected it to be much lighter, but it was not. Despite the weight and the abrupt design, Lamborghini sold 177 copies of the original version. One of the interesting features of the Jarama were the swivel-down headlight covers (*above*).

performance was still plenty high. The trouble was, it didn't seem quite as high as it should have been. Again, exact numbers differ, but many thought Lamborghini's latest 2+2 to be incapable of its claimed 162-mph maximum, and most everyone believed fuel consumption was excessive.

It is important to avoid dismissal of the Jarama as either a disappointment or a failure. Purists didn't find it as thrilling as its two sisters, but it wasn't meant to be. Like the Islero before it and the Touring-bodied GTs before that, the Jarama was supposed to be conservative. Again, the driver Ferruccio Lamborghini had in mind was one much like himself—a prosperous, more mature enthusiast who needed a genuinely fast yet easy-to-drive car for long-distance business travel. As ever, *Il Cavaliere* was not one of those at Sant'Agata pressuring for show-off hot rods.

In fact, there was evidently much to like about the Jarama. Even those who

didn't much care for the styling appreciated the airy thin-pillar roofline and the adequate rear headroom it provided. (However, rear legroom in early models was next to nil.) Equally practical were fold-down rear seatbacks for extra cargo space.

Although naturally as wide as the Espada, the Jarama was trimmer in length and thus felt more compact on the road. At the same time, it offered the same combination of fine road manners and ride. "On the road it was a very nice car," agreed Jean-Francois Marchet, "with truly excellent suspension behavior, both comfortable and efficient in cornering and without noticeable roll."

Britain's *Motor* tempered its praise with a list of unfortunate first impressions, citing "poor driving position, heavy steering and indifferently-planned cockpit" and poor interior finish. However, the editors found that "soon these things are overshadowed, if never eliminated, by other more

agreeable qualities like the superb ride, which puts to shame that of many luxury saloons, let alone other sports cars. The roadholding is also outstanding. . . . The performance is exciting, the noise exhilarating, the brakes and stability at speed superb."

In fact, *Motor*'s report centered on the fine roadability and ride of the car: "At speed the Jarama is impressively stable, maintaining an arrow-straight course at its natural cruising gait of 130 mph. . . . The suspension combines those desirable but usually incompatible qualities of resilience for soaking up the bumps, and firmness to minimize wallow and roll."

England's *CAR* also lauded the Jarama's dynamic qualities. Ride was termed "absorbent yet responsive," handling as "beautifully balanced" despite the evident nose-heavy weight distribution. "Indeed, the latest car is as precise in its handling as the original 350 GT, which is saying something, as the original model was superior

Though the Jarama shares many design elements with the Espada, the wheelbase was shortened 10.6 inches. The S version, which was released in 1973, sported engine compartment cooling vents aft of the front tires (*top*). The hood was also altered and the wheels became bolt-ons instead of knock-offs. In an effort to improve performance, the engine of the Jarama S (*above*) was also revised.

Wallace makes a statement

As with the Miura, Wallace created a one-off of the Jarama. He may have been unhappy with the direction Lamborghini was taking; and during 1972, to show his feelings, he turned one Jarama into a hot rod. "We had a lack of things to do, I guess," he explains facetiously.

Wallace first went through the bodyshell with a welding torch to add stiffness and remounted the engine a few inches rearward to improve weight distribution. The cabin was stripped of all unnecessary equipment, a rollover bar was installed and the backseat area was filled with fuel tanks. Outside, he attached lighter body panels, including aluminum doors, and substituted plastic for glass in the windows. Bumpers were scrapped, a racing-type chin spoiler went up front, the stock hood was swapped for a special item with radiator air extractors, headlights were moved down, and a quick-fill fuel cap stuck through the rear window. Wheels were Miura-type Campagnolos.

Bob doesn't recall the exact numbers, but this Jarama "was quite a bit lighter" than stock. Quite a bit faster, too. A racer's grin twists his lips as he remembers: "The thing was quicker than stink off the line!"

That, he was trying to say, was what a Lamborghini should be.

It was clear that Bob Wallace was unhappy with the Jarama, and he took time out to build his own version. This personalized Jarama GTS (*above*) has lighter body panels, a roll-over cage, spoilers, and a special hood.

to each of its successors in this respect...."

Observing how well the rear wheels maintained contact on bumpy roads, *CAR* credited the efficient suspension design, calling the Espada/Jarama geometry "a considerable advance" on that of previous Lamborghinis. "The wide-based double wishbones...are arranged to give more or less constant wheel alignment from bump to rebound," aided by the constant-velocity rear-halfshaft joints. This sophistication helped the "monster" 215-section tires (wider than the Espada's) stick to the road like lint on velvet, making it "surprisingly difficult to get the tail out even in the lower gears."

Despite many glowing reports, it would be wrong to gloss over the car's shortcomings. Many road tests agreed with *Motor*'s: The Jarama was indeed flawed.

For instance, those wide treads and the lack of power steering made parking an arm-wrestle. Everyone mentioned it, although some added that steering effort and feel were just fine at speed. As *CAR* said, steering that grows lighter with speed is "an incentive to get a move on if ever there was one."

Move off the straight-and-narrow and the higher cornering forces generated by the better tires and suspension revealed inadequate lateral location in the Jarama's seats. Some drivers complained they couldn't see the widely spaced tach and speedometer with both hands on the steering wheel, and the low, centrally mounted clock was hidden by the shifter. Marchet found the dash-mounted wipe/wash controls "nearly invisible at night, requiring much memory and the touch of a blind man."

The Jarama's climate control was something of a contradiction in terms. The system provided both cool and warm air simultaneously, and its levers sometimes didn't seem to control anything, including the defroster. Also, the fixed rear side glass dictated opening a door window for ventilation—hardly conducive to 130-mph cruising.

Like the Espada, the Jarama also suffered from a low driving position. So despite narrower pillars and a "vast" windshield, some felt its outward vision was just as difficult. One tester complained that the parked wipers

The Jarama S (*above*) was designed to be a businessman's cruiser, however cooling problems forced the installation of a very un-business-like scoop on the top of the hood. The interior also received major alterations. Dashboard layout (*below*) was revised—though speedo and tach were still on opposite ends of the dash. Also, aluminum trim replaced wood pieces, seatbacks were thinned to increase rear seat room, and switchgear was better labeled.

Power improvements on the Jarama S brought top speed up to a tested 161 mph, and lowered 0-60 mph times to 6.5 seconds. Soon after its launch, power steering became standard equipment. One curious option was a Chrysler three-speed automatic. This transmission mated so poorly with the V-12's powerband that even under full-throttle acceleration the transmission would shift into the next gear before the engine reached its torque peak—maximum horsepower was still 2000 rpm away from that!

actually obscured his view. In addition, the rounded front fenders dropped away from sight and made it hard to judge lateral clearances in this wide car.

The list of liabilities seemed endless: ill-fitting carpets and poorly finished dash wood, seats that would jump their tracks if adjusted too far forward, sluggish cold starting on one car, overheating in traffic because one or the other of the electric radiator fans didn't work, complete failure of all lights on one test run, doors that wouldn't stay open and were hard to close, a curious under-dash handle marked "start" that actually released the hood.

To top it all off, the car had an awkward pedal and steering wheel arrangement. *CAR* said, "it is sad to see that Lamborghini's development staff have...caught the malignant Italian disease that causes the legs to shrink." The steering wheel was adjustable, but only with wrench work.

Despite all of the criticism, the car tested very well. Try 0-60 mph in 6.8 seconds and a standing quarter-mile of 14.9 seconds at an estimated 95 mph. That was for a European model, but *Road & Track*'s U.S.-spec sample wasn't far adrift. Reportedly weighing 3600 pounds at the curb and 3865 pounds as tested (53/47 percent front/rear) it

clocked 0-60 in 7.2 seconds and ran the standing-quarter in 15.6 at 97 mph. This was with the lower 4.5:1 axle ratio (vs. 4.09), which limited top speed to "only" 152 mph at 7050 rpm. On the skidpad, *R&T*'s Jarama pulled 0.81 g— a very impressive number for a car of that era.

It is truly too bad that the Jarama's build failed to live up to expectations, for the car had the specs and speed to match any number of 1990-era supercars. Though a 3600-pound curb weight may have seemed excessive then, it doesn't now.

For all its faults, the Jarama was redeemed, as *Motor* noted, by its open-road performance. "Stroke that long, silky-smooth gas pedal and all the quibbles were drowned in the V-12's howl." This howl could reach 100 decibels on a sound meter, according to *R&T* (which makes you wonder what happened to the "quiet GT" Ferruccio envisioned), but to anyone with "Blood of the Miura" in the arteries, the sound was glorious.

Jarama production spanned a period of economic turmoil and inflation, so price figures are problematic. However, *R&T* put the Jarama's 1972 U.S. list at $22,625, including dealer prep. That compared to $23,750 for a Ferrari Daytona and $22,515 for Maserati's

Ghibli. All, incidentally, are about four times what a Chevy Corvette cost in those days.

As with the Islero, Lamborghini eventually found it necessary to revise the Jarama quite heavily. Thus, after 177 first-generation cars came the "S" or "400 GTS" model, which saw 150 copies. Presented at Geneva in 1972, the Jarama S predictably claimed more horsepower: a total of 365, up by 15 bhp, thanks mainly to a more efficient exhaust system, according to Wallace. Heads, cams, and carburetion also were revised. The official factory numbers suggest that the S was substantially lighter than the first-series Jarama without explaining why, but Wallace says it's not true. In any case, the extra power supposedly lifted top speed to a genuine 161 mph.

More important from the customer's viewpoint was a revised interior featuring slimmer front seatbacks that left more leg space behind, and a reworked instrument panel with better switchgear labeling and trim made of aluminum instead of wood. Heat and noise insulation was said to be improved. Soon after, launch power steering became standard equipment. It made parking easier, but some felt it detracted from high-speed stability. Later still, one could specify Chrysler

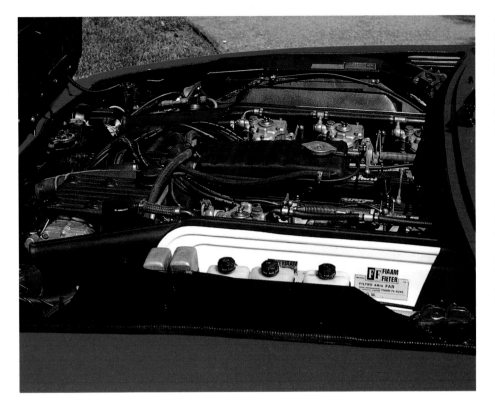

With minor tuning to the exhaust system and camshaft revisions, the familiar Lamborghini 3.9-liter V-12 (*left*) put out 365 bhp in the Jarama S. The car's high weight and poor balance hurt performance. In an effort to better distribute the weight, the battery was moved to the trunk. By the time production of the Jarama ceased, over 300 copies had been built. Not bad for a car that lived in the shadow of the Miura and Countach.

three-speed TorqueFlite automatic and a pair of narrow, removable roof panels, but neither option garnered many orders.

A Jarama S was easy to spot by its prominent hood scoop between the existing NACA ducts, and new outlets on the front-fender sides, one behind each wheel arch. Both helped move more air through the engine compartment to keep it cooler. Closer examination revealed parallel-action windshield wipers that parked to starboard, replacing the Espada-style arrangement where the left blade rested above the right one. Completing "S" exterior changes were slightly revised bumpers and new five-bolt wheels borrowed from the Espada.

The Jarama S was even more misunderstood than the original. While it was faster, better finished, and roomier than most of its competitors, the public tried to make the car do too many things. What it did best was cruise with distinction, and, when called upon, run away from the pack. The Miura and Espada were the attention-getters in the Lamborghini stable.

"For it is only, I promise you," said the writer for *CAR*, "when you start to thrash a car like this, to belt it and boot it and cane the living daylights out of the poor inanimate thing, that it really comes alive and demonstrates what it is to have so much investment, so much skill and so much faith built in with every loving twist of every nut and bolt." The Jarama had all that and more.

model	1970-73 Jarama	1973-76 Jarama S
production	177	150
engine	dohc V-12	dohc V-12
displacement cc/ci	3929/240	3929/240
horsepower @ RPM (DIN)	350 @ 7500	365 @ 7500
torque @ RPM (lbs/ft)	280 @ 5500	280 @ 5500
length (mm/in.)	4485/174.9	4485/174.9
width (mm/in.)	1820/71	1820/71
height (mm/in.)	1190/46.4	1190/46.4
wheelbase (mm/in.)	2380/92.8	2380/92.8
track, front (mm/in.)	1490/58.1	1490/58.1
track, rear (mm/in.)	1490/58.1	1490/58.1
weight (kg/lbs)[1]	1540/3388	1460/3212

[1]Factory dry-weight claims, actual numbers higher.

39

CHAPTER FIVE

MIURA

FERRUCCIO LAMBORGHINI HAD

ALWAYS CLAIMED TO BE

UNINTERESTED IN RACING AND

SAID HE WOULD NEVER BUILD

A RACE CAR. THE CHASSIS HE

SHOWED AT THE 1965 TURIN SHOW

SAID OTHERWISE, AND WOULD

LEAD TO A CAR THAT CHANGED

THE HISTORY OF LAMBORGHINI.

No one could have predicted the sensation caused by the prototype chassis Lamborghini unveiled at the 1965 Turin auto show. A product of a year's worth of secret development work, the chassis was somewhat of an experiment for Lamborghini. Any car that would be placed on top of it was unnamed, and work had not even begun on a design for its body. Given the GTV's premature showing, you'd think Ferruccio wouldn't have presented his new sports car until it was completely ready. However, this time his impatience did not hurt.

Aboard the chassis was a V-12 displacing 3929 cubic centimeters and bristling with four camshafts and a dozen intake stacks—remember that the 350 GTV carried only a bunch of ceramic tiles under its hood. That the Miura's engine sat both amidships *and* side-saddle only enhanced the mystery and surprise. The monocoque was festooned with lightening holes for all to see. Like art that leaves much to the imagination and thus is most fascinating, this chassis created the wildest of daydreams—and would-be owners started waving fat checkbooks. There was no question: even without a body, it had more sex appeal than anything else on show.

Yet up to this point, the new supercar had not really been an important project at Lamborghini. While the company's cadre of hotbloods was quite serious about it and Ferruccio himself was enthusiastic, in terms of funding and corporate priorities it was essentially a promotional exercise, just something to attract buyers. Production was feasible, but nobody at Sant'Agata thought it would amount to more than a handful.

Now, at Turin, Ferruccio found himself besieged by eager buyers. He couldn't resist taking a stack of firm orders—for a car that wasn't even a fully finished prototype, let alone ready for production.

In a mere four months Ferruccio and his team had most of the development done. The biggest step was body design; however, it was the easiest of all. Perhaps remembering the aesthetic disaster the GTV had been, Ferruccio wanted this one to be right the first time. Touring, which had been responsible for the production 350/400 GTs, was going out of business and thus unavailable. However, every coachbuilder in Italy was clamoring to clothe the spectacular new chassis, so Lamborghini had his pick. He settled on *Carrozzeria* Nuccio Bertone. There, a young stylist named Marcello Gandini set out to design the body.

Styling is one thing, melding appearance with function quite another.

Bertone worked closely with Lamborghini, each clearly understanding the other's problems and sharing the same ambitions. What they constructed was not only one of the most beautiful automobiles ever conceived, but a true work of art.

It was completed, or at least assembled, just in time for the March 1966 Geneva salon. Done in a startling orange-red set off by black trim, the production prototype caused the same stir its bare chassis had in Turin the previous fall. Thus, Ferruccio Lamborghini suddenly found his name on the lips of wealthy and powerful people everywhere. He had done this just three years after establishing himself as a boutique automaker to the wealthy.

The car had a model designation by the time it reached Switzerland—P 400. The number represented the now-familiar 4.0-liter displacement (in deciliters). P denoted *posteriore*, though here it meant a midships engine. Ferruccio also thought his latest should also have a proper name. The resulting label, Miura, not only related to his birth sign, Taurus, but referred to one of the most respected of Spanish fighting bulls: the ferocious breed of Don Eduardo Miura.

Astonishingly beautiful, technically advanced, and unbelievably rapid, the

Miura was a dream come true: a road car built in the image of the latest mid-engine racing machines. It shook up the sports-car establishment like nothing else before and put "Lamborghini" right up there with "Ferrari" in the hearts and minds of enthusiasts everywhere.

In many senses, the seed for the Miura was planted in 1964. Lamborghini's first production model, the 350 GT, had been well received upon its launch the year before and had settled into steady production. Refining it was all Lamborghini needed to do to cement his reputation as an automaker. Although it was solid and speedy, the 350 was conventional and not very exciting. *Automobili Ferruccio Lamborghini* was in danger of becoming just another purveyor of GT cars in a Europe already filled with them. Ferruccio needed an image car.

In the autumn of '64, as one story goes, Sant'Agata's key triumvirate— Giampaolo Dallara, Paolo Stanzani,

Without a doubt the most distinctive production automobile of its time, the Miura P 400 bowed to no one the road. The Miura (*above*) rocked the automotive world during its introduction at the 1966 Turin auto show. Fitted with two seats, the car was a step away from Ferruccio's dream of a luxury sports car, however, driving it was a leap into the future. Quad cams, four carburetors, twelve cylinders, and 350 horsepower made the world go by in fast forward.

and Bob Wallace—found they had a little time for daydreaming. "Here we have this fine new factory and this fabulous new V-12," they likely mused. "Wouldn't it be great if the boss let us build a race car?"

The story is much cloudier than that, but luckily Wallace was there: "You've got to remember that back then we three were just part of a whole very good design crew there...a whole bunch of young but very gifted designers and draftsmen—very, very enthusiastic young kids. Initially there was no one in the technical office over the age of 25. We'd sit down in the evenings, probably eight or 10 of us, and kick it over about building a rear-engine car, because we felt that everything that was on the market, including the 350, design-wise, was antiquated."

So the story that the Miura sprang from just "three musketeers" is an oversimplification, much like the story about the three creating a pure racing car.

"I've always been a firm believer in racing," Wallace answers. "Stanzani was very enthusiastic about racing. How deep his involvement would have been, I don't know, but he was always very enthusiastic about it. Dallara was crazy about it, and so were most of the other kids. So in our minds, we had hoped to make a race car as well. But Lamborghini was adamant. In fact, he was the only person there with enough common sense to not divide up the factory's efforts."

Ferruccio Lamborghini, at age 48, was too careful to risk capital on the uncertainties of the track—remember his first and only attempt at racing ended up in disappointment. True, arch rival Enzo Ferrari had built much of his reputation on racing, but he'd been in the game for decades. Then too, Ferruccio was concerned (as he revealed years later) that son Tonino might take his involvement as a green flag for a competition driving career of

his own. No, thanks: Ferruccio would not go down Racer Road.

Wallace justifies the decision by pointing to the sad case of ATS, the tiny Italian maker of racing and road cars. ATS was formed by some of those who broke from Ferrari in 1961. "They started out with gobs of money and some very good designers [with] very good ideas," he recalls. "Then they divided everything up into two abortive programs and ended up with no money and not doing anything anyway."

So though Ferruccio's youngsters might have dreamed of building a racer, they knew that they'd have to build a street machine first and that it would necessarily be the basis for a racing Lamborghini—should the boss ever approve one. And, of course, for the racer to have any chance for success, its road-car parent would have to be outstanding.

As for the oft-told tale of enthusiastic young conspirators working on this supercar in secret, Bob replies that the boss knew what they were up to all along. "Basically, he was involved pretty much right from the beginning. We'd actually ask him, 'Can we pursue something like this?' and he'd say, 'Yup.' We'd go back to him when we had some concrete proposals, something pretty much 90-percent clear as to what was going to be done. And he was all for it right from the start."

What's significant here is that Ferruccio had clearly changed his mind about not building a purely technical car. Far from discouraging his spirited crew, he gave them free reign of his sparkling new factory to realize something very close to their dream.

"Okay," he might have said, tapping their drawings, "I won't authorize a race car, but I'll let you build a car as much like a race car as it can be and still be a good street car. I'll let you build

While engine displacement was still 3929 cc, almost everything else was new (*right*). Most notable were the four downdraft Webers, and the entirely new block/transmission casting. This transmission sat along the right side of the engine and shared lubrication with the engine. Because of this compact package interior room (*below*) was surprisingly good. Controls were directly in front of the driver and the passenger was given grab handles and a foot rest.

the most technically advanced sports car in the world." He might not have admitted it aloud, but he'd surely concluded that a such no-holds-barred machine would enhance his firm's performance image without risking a thing.

So the engineers refocused and set about applying their knowledge of racing design to create the fastest, most advanced, most exciting road car they

could imagine. That meant joining the mid-engine revolution that was then changing the shape of international motorsports.

Putting power behind the people was an idea as old as the automobile itself, and a small number of designers had revived it from time to time for both racing and road use. However, it never really took hold despite the likes of the all-conquering Auto Union Grand Prix

cars of the 1930s and their spiritual descendants, the giant-killing Porsche 356s and 550 Spyders of the '50s.

The early '50s also saw Cooper of England start to make its mark on the racetracks of Europe with small-displacement, mid-engine single-seaters. The tiny specialist firm relentlessly kept fitting ever-larger engines, step by step, until its 2.5-liter, 180-mph GP car won the Formula 1 World Championship in 1959. Cooper repeated as champion the following year.

That was the breakthrough. The news that a race car worked better with its engine behind the cockpit and ahead of the rear axle spread rapidly, and most everyone designing racers of any type or size were soon doing "middies." The layout enabled a more compact power package to be situated more closely to the vehicle's dynamic centers of roll and gravity for flatter, faster cornering. It also allowed a more compact, aerodynamic vehicle that was accordingly more agile and better able to put its power to the road.

In 1959, Cooper also built an open-cockpit sports-racer, the Monaco, along the lines of its winning F1 design. British rival Lotus followed the next year with its similar Monte Carlo. Then, in 1961, Italy's venerated Maserati unleashed its Tipo 63, a curvaceous, open sports-racer carrying a massive 3.0-liter V-12 amidships. It was bold but unsuccessful. Wallace, who worked on it, terms the 63 "the most abominable thing you've ever seen in your life."

It was also in seminal '61 that neighboring Ferrari unveiled its mid-engine

246SP. Powered by a healthy little 2.4-liter V-6, it worked well enough to win races, prompting Ferrari to design a similar chassis around its classic 3.0-liter Testa Rossa V-12. The resulting 250 P of 1963 worked even better, becoming the first mid-engine machine to win the prestigious 24 Hours of Le Mans. An evolutionary successor claimed outright victory in '64, and a coupe version, the 250 LM, would do the same in '65.

Meantime, very early in 1963, the tiny English firm of Lola had unwrapped a sleek little GT coupe designed around American "small-block" V-8 engines (which seemed quite large in Europe). This Lola GT caught the eye of Ford Motor Company, then charging ahead with its "Total Performance" assault on most every form of motorsports worldwide. With Lola's help, the U.S. giant developed this basic car into the Ford GT40, a landmark design that first raced in May 1964 and, in later forms, would win Le Mans four years running (1966-69).

The GT40's true stature was not yet apparent in late '64, but its design had impressed Lamborghini's Dallara, who

began drawing up a similar layout. Of course, he was no amateur sketching a dream car but a professional designer starting first from principles.

The car he and his two "co-conspirators" wanted to build would have been primarily a competition machine like the 250 LM and GT40. As the state of the racing art hadn't yet seen sports racers entirely removed from the old dual-purpose, "race-and-ride" ideal, both the Ferrari and Ford could also be—and were—driven on the road. On the other hand, neither was at all roomy, comfortable, or easy to live with—in short, not very practical. And while the look of these "GT Prototypes" had enthusiasts drooling, no one had yet come up with an honest, powerful mid-engine road car in the same mold. Lamborghini would.

Dallara worked from the inside out. His 350 GT chassis was a steel-tube structure (like the Ferrari LM's), but race car builders were turning to a more advanced type of construction inspired by aircraft practice. This naturally appealed to Dallara, who had trained as an aeronautical engineer, remember. The new mid-engine Lam-

As with most Lamborghinis, the Miura was not without its faults. So, in 1969 the P 400 S was introduced (*top*). While retaining the same inspired exterior design, air conditioning, electrically operated windows, and new Pirelli P 70 tires were added. Ahead of the driver sat the spare tire, battery, and radiator (*above, far left*). Horsepower was also up—to 370 at 7700 rpm—due to new camshafts, and the interior included a lockable glove box (*above*). The car's top speed was now in excess of 170 mph and 140 mph could be reached within 30 seconds.

borghini would thus employ a GT40-like unitized or monocoque hull, light but enormously strong and fabricated of sheet steel, which was then more practical for this purpose than aluminum. As on the Ford, the roof would be integral with the structure and front and rear body sections would be separate, unstressed panels—in effect, just hinged covers; the radiator and spare wheel would nestle under the front panel. Suspension would be all-independent, of course, and Lamborghini would naturally use its "stock-block" engine.

At this point, we can imagine Dallara sitting back and chewing his pencil. It was time to strike out on his own. The GT40 was magnificent for its mission, but the Lamborghini was to be a very different animal: not meant to lap a track quickly but to carry people happily.

Designers of single-seat race cars had found that mid-engine positioning facilitated driver positioning, because drivetrain components didn't intrude on cockpit space, and the driver's legs fit naturally into the space between the front wheels. Laying out a two-seat middie was more of a challenge because the cockpit would have to be wider to accommodate an extra set of legs.

There were two obvious ways around this: an extra-long wheelbase, to put the front wheels further ahead of the cockpit; the other was to mount the seats very close together. The latter was preferable for a racer, but the travelling companion of a wealthy person (the new Lamborghini wouldn't be cheap) would not take kindly to crawling across a foot of chassis structure, rubbing shoulders with the driver, or squeezing legs into a narrow, angled tunnel. GT40 passengers endured all of this.

A longer wheelbase wasn't the way to go, either. The new Lamborghini was supposed to be at least as agile as the GT40, which spanned 95 inches

between wheel centers. Yet the Lamborghini V-12 was long: 43 inches with clutch and other accessories—almost twice the length of the GT40's longitudinally situated 90-degree V-8. If Dallara weren't careful with packaging, his mid-engine sports car would end up having the looks, handling, and mass of a truck.

New approaches were clearly needed. Wallace says that the first considered was a three-seat arrangement: "Our car initially was pretty well drawn up as a central-seater, three-seater car." The one-off Ferrari 365 P of 1966 showed how it might have worked. Driver's seat, steering wheel, and pedals would have been in the middle. Given sufficient cockpit width, this would have left room for two flanking seats near enough to the doors that passengers wouldn't have to clamber in very far. And once installed, they'd have adequate foot room despite wheel-arch intrusion.

Such "1+2" seating might have been acceptable given reasonably athletic owner/drivers; it certainly would have attracted the desired attention to the new Lamborghini. But the idea just didn't seem right somehow, and it never even reached Ferruccio's desk. "We'd seen ourselves that it was impractical," Wallace recalls. "I think we had someone make a one-to-five scale model of the body, or something like that. But that was all. It was a real

Behind the engine sat a usable trunk (*above*). Oddly, this tilted up with the rear body assembly when engine access was required. Though styling changed very little on the P 400 S, chrome now surrounded the headlights and the front and side windows.

wild-looking thing, but it was scrapped as being completely impractical as a road car."

Besides, Ferruccio's charges had stumbled on a much better idea. In pushing some spare parts around on a big, sturdy tabletop, they suddenly realized that their V-12 measured only 21 inches across its widest point. It could go in sideways! "Just kicking things around, moving all the units around on a chassis table, keeping it within a certain wheelbase and a certain cockpit size that we wanted and so forth, the transverse engine came up and sort of snowballed from there."

With that, everything else literally fell into place. And such an elegant solution: The sideways engine made for a more compact powertrain that allowed the entire cockpit to be behind the front wheel wells, so foot room was no problem and occupants could ride comfortably apart within a manageable 97-inch wheelbase (on the prototype). That was two inches longer than the GT40 span but three shorter than that of the 350 GT.

There was still the puzzle of how to get the drive to the rear wheels, but that was a problem for everybody in those pioneering mid-engine days. Lamborghini would have to build its own transaxle anyway, so it might as well be a specialized one, mounted at the "rear" of the engine—in unit with the crankcase, in fact, just like a motorcycle gearbox. "That was to make the whole thing much more compact," Wallace observes, "to keep the whole engine and transmission within a certain size and therefore have room for the driver and also fit everything in a certain wheelbase."

Some people hailed this as a radical new concept. However, Wallace doesn't view the Miura that way: "Just an overgrown Morris Mini-Minor," he says with a grin. The Mini, of course, was a tiny front-drive econobox with a small inline four, but midships-transverse positioning was a perfectly logical layout with numerous precedents. In fact, that same year—1964—Honda campaigned its first Formula 1 car, a 1.5-liter V-12 job of exactly this configuration.

Wallace had already seen something quite like this during his time at Maserati: "It was done by Giulio Alfieri on a shoestring, when there was a dollar or two to spare. He put [the engine] on a dyno occasionally. It

never went into a car, and Maserati was very secretive about it. When the Honda transverse V-12 came out, it was virtually identical, so much so it seems strange. But it's not that unusual for different design teams to come up with very similar designs."

The Austin/Morris Mini appeared in 1959, but transverse engines weren't news even then. Bugatti's last racer had run four years before with a rear-mounted crosswise straight eight, and early Coopers wore their motorcycle engines the same way. Among road cars, at least one, the little French-built de Dion Bouton, had an "east-west" engine as early as the turn of the century.

The fact that the Miura's layout was merely a refinement of existing technology clearly didn't diminish its wondrousness. And that other stylists had created swoopy bodywork certainly couldn't dim the drama of its shape.

Bertone broke the team-design tradition for the Miura and instead assigned one main creative spark, a young man about the same age as Dallara, Stanzani, and Wallace. Marcello Gandini was 25 in 1965, and what sprang from his drawing board was a young man's sports car: lithe, energetic, and sensuous. Overall, it was somewhat reminiscent of the GT40 that had so impressed Dallara. Instead of the

Ford's rather utilitarian lines, the car Gandini drew was so sweetly harmonious, so boldly imaginative, so exquisitely alive that it remains fresh decades later. Indeed, this automobile has long since gone down as a design tour de force.

No man is an island, however, and at least two elements of the eventual production Miura could well have been inspired by the work of an equally talented Gandini colleague. This was none other than Giorgio Giugiaro, already winning fame with designs like the neat little Sprint coupe body that Bertone was starting to build for Alfa, and destined to move on to Ghia (where he'd pen masterworks like the Maserati Ghibli) before setting up his own firm, Ital Design.

In his earlier Bertone days Giugiaro had styled the Testudo, a striking one-off fastback based on Chevrolet Corvair running gear that toured the inter-

Many people thought the vents around the pop-up headlights (*below*) of the P 400 looked like eyelashes. To avoid overheating, fresh air was drawn in through the front of the car and out through the vents on the top of the hood. Coupled with this was an angled radiator with dual electric cooling fans. The angled radiator allowed for a much lower front end.

national show circuit in 1963. The name roughly translated as "turtle" in Italian, but no turtle ever looked like this: sleek, low, and rather wide, with a very long, shapely snout and a rounded, substantial rump (which may have prompted the name). Its most radical feature was a huge front-hinged canopy-cum-doors with side windows fully wrapped from B-pillar to B-pillar and no windshield posts. The side glass swept up at the canopy's trailing edges inboard of vertical slots that fed air to the rear-mounted Corvair flat six. The Miura's midships V-12 would be served in almost exactly the same way.

The Testudo headlamp treatment was equally predictive: dual round units that "reclined" flush with the nose when switched off and snapped to attention when switched on. This idea also resurfaced on the Miura—to such a striking effect that Porsche was likely moved to copy it for the 928, initiated in the early Seventies, the Miura's twilight years.

The engine/transaxle package, however, was extremely complex to make. To a draftsman it was mere artwork, just a matter of lines on paper. But to the people running Lamborghini's foundry it presented a three-dimensional problem of major proportions. "Back then, doing a one-piece casting of that size was difficult," says Wallace. "There were a lot of bugs to iron out."

Then there was the method chosen for making the bodyshells, especially the aluminum front and rear hinged

sections. "All that panel work was done with locally reinforced resin dies. They won't do a production run of more than 200, 240 units." Eventually, the Miura would sell nearly that many copies in a single year.

Lamborghini wasn't the first outfit to underestimate demand for a complex automobile, and the consequences of this fundamental error would dog Miura production from start to finish. As Wallace observes: "The car was costing a fortune to build because of the inadequate tooling for it, and that's why the cost of reproducing body parts for them today is enormous."

One final factor that complicated the building stage was similar to a problem encountered with the 350 GTV: the fact that there were early thoughts of a competition Miura. While Wallace and his colleagues probably knew this was just a pipe dream, others in the organization were openly and officially predicting it. For instance, a June 24, 1966, press release from Lamborghini's

eastern U.S. distributor promised that the new Miura "will be in production this fall in two models, one for the road and one for the track." That fall timetable was equally optimistic by no less than six months.

Further, though less direct evidence that a racing Miura was at least contemplated is seen in the first four-color Miura brochure put out by Lamborghini's *Ufficio Stampa e Propaganda* (Office of Press and Public Relations). On the back cover was a spec chart in four languages listing "Maximum speed: 300 Km/h road version." Granted, road version appeared only in the English section, so Italian, French, and German readers who couldn't read English missed this clear implication that there was something else. But inside, over a photo of the original Miura engine with multi-plate clutch, is a statement that "the house" offers two models—*La casa ne offre due versioni: normale (350 cavalli DIN); spinto* ["pushed"] *(430 cavalli DIN)*."

On that last point, Wallace says nothing so grand as 430 horsepower was ever extracted from a 4.0-liter Lamborghini V-12 (not even the one in his Jota hot rod). Even 350 bhp was very optimistic for an early Miura; 320 was more like it. In any case, however strong the impulse to build a racing P 400, it weakened. All efforts were concentrated on the production car.

Not counting the bare chassis shown at Turin '65 (which was just a mockup, never bodied, and ultimately scrapped) the orange Geneva car was Miura No. 1. This hand-built prototype was soon subjected to exhaustive tests on the roads and tracks of Italy to exterminate the bugs in its basic design.

It was hard work, but also a little fun. Two months after its triumphant splash in Switzerland, the orange Miura was guest of honor in Monaco,

Rolling test bed, race car, or toy?

Another unofficial Miura (though built at Sant'Agata) was called Jota. A one-off custom, it was the most ambitious of Bob Wallace's personal Lamborghinis.

Jota is the letter "J" in Italian. Here it referred to Appendix J, a section of the international auto-racing rules in force around early 1970. Yes, racing. No more fooling around for Wallace. He wanted to go racing, he wanted Lamborghini to go racing, and this "J car" was conceived as a flat-out P 400 racer. But he never actually proposed that it be raced. "No. I knew that was a waste of time."

It would be logical to assume, as some have, that the Jota was a test bed for the changes to come on the following year's Miura SV, but Wallace denies this: "It was useful for tire testing, and it also acted as a, call it stimulation, for the design office, but it had no real practical bearing on any of the production cars. It was basically just a toy of mine.

This particular "toy" was recognizably Miura-based, but few elements were left untouched. The basic steel chassis was given a new floor made of aircraft aluminum, and more of the lightweight stuff was used in the body, whose fender profiles were distinctly more aggressive than stock. The pop-up headlights were discarded for fixed units under plastic fairings, a "moustache" type front spoiler was added, large air vents were cut in behind the front wheels, the normal dual windshield wipers gave way to a single large blade with racing-type parallelogram action, and side windows changed from glass to lightweight plastic sheeting, fixed but incorporating small sliding hatches for ventilation. The interior was naturally stripped to the bone, bereft of central console and all normal trim. Also, where the

Miura's brake and clutch pedals mounted to the floor, the Jota's hung from competition-style master cylinders above the footwell.

The Miura's suspension geometry was reworked for the Jota to accommodate very broad-shouldered tires on lightweight non-standard wheels measuring nine inches wide fore and 12 inches aft. To improve weight distribution, Wallace replaced the front-mounted fuel tank with a smaller one in each door sill (shades of GT40) and moved the spare wheel to just behind the engine. In all, the Jota ended up some 800 pounds lighter than the stock Miura—about 1950 pounds.

Wallace also hopped up the engine, of course, boosting compression to 11.5:1, fitting wilder cams and electronic ignition, separating the crankcase and transmission oil supplies, rigging a dry-sump lubrication system, and adding a competition exhaust system that terminated in a quartet of megaphones. Some very elevated horsepower figures have been printed for the Jota, but honest dyno testing, according to Bob himself, showed about 418 bhp at 8000 rpm.

The Jota was not Wallace's personal property, and once cash began running low, Lamborghini management saw it as a disposable asset. "It had a fairly short life," says the man who put so much of himself into it. "The factory had financial problems, and it ended up being sold to a rich industrialist up in Brescia. His mechanic took it out with his girlfriend on a Saturday night, and ripped out the side fuel cell against a freeway bridge. The car caught fire, burnt to the ground, and that's it."

The loss was a sad one for Lamborghini enthusiasts, and a few rushed to make up for it by turning their cars into Jota replicas.

serving as the ceremonial circuit-opener at the single most important race on the Grand Prix calendar. It was another Lamborghini front-page production. Wallace drove the car over from Italy the day before the race and in the evening parked it in the absolute center of rich-and-famous activity, Casino Square in front of the Hotel de Paris.

Thus began another Lamborghini legend. According to Pete Coltrin, within seconds people were gathered five deep around the lovely, exotic piece of rolling sculpture. Ferruccio himself, watching from the outskirts, waited for the strategic moment; then, on the pretext of showing the car to one of his industry friends, made his way through the throng, opened the door, climbed in and fired the engine. The crowd instantly swelled to 10 deep.

"Lamborghini himself was pretty much a showman," remembers Wallace with a smile. "He'd get in it and rev the hell out of the thing, scream it around the block. We also gave it to one of the Italian drivers, I think it was [Lodovico] Scarfiotti, to do some hot night laps around the track.

"Yeah, Monte Carlo was when it really woke Ferrari up to something, because Agnelli [Gianni, chairman of Fiat] had one of the Ferrari engineers with him, and just pulled him out of the hotel and showed it to him. 'You people better wake up!' he says. Yeah, it caused quite a sensation."

But there wasn't much time for crowd-stopping, because the test schedule was grueling for a single "mule." Actually, a second prototype was completed, a mustard-yellow car, but test-driver Wallace says it was used more for show. That one, Miura No. 2, survives today. The original car unfortunately does not. It was destroyed.

Wallace recounts the sad tale. "Someone drove it up to Bertone's one day, on business, and was on his way back when he stopped at a stoplight. He was sitting there when he saw the wheels of this truck climbing up the back bodywork. All he could do was bail out and watch it happen."

Some historians believe a third prototype was built to the original configuration, but Wallace says no. The third car built was to final production specs, and getting to that point involved important changes.

The engine/transaxle package was altered in two ways. First, the original

Bob Wallace was at it again, but this time it was on company money. His Jota was a rolling test bed for factory updates to the Miura. Several of his changes appeared on the final version of the Miura, the P 400 SV.

clutch was an exposed three-plate design mounted on the input end of the gearbox, much like a typical motorcycle clutch. This gave way to a more conventional, single-plate enclosed unit at the end of the crankshaft (on the car's left). However, the clutch was still cantilevered out, or overhung, to extend beyond the geartrain that took drive to the transaxle. The flywheel and clutch pressure-plate were overhung extensions of the crank and were moving elements—"just an overgrown Mini-Minor," as Wallace says.

A second change concerned the direction of crank rotation. In the Lamborghini V-12, like most auto engines, the shaft turned clockwise as seen from the front. With the engine situated 90 degrees, clutch-end to the car's left, the crank thus revolved in the same direction as the road wheels. This was reversed on all production Miuras so that the crank rotated "backwards."

Wallace explains that these two changes were intimately related: "The first engine had an external, race-type clutch, and it was completely impractical for a road car. There were a lot of ideas that were impractical. We had a chain drive in there at one stage, like an Olds Toronado. When we had a train of gears, we had lubrication problems, you name it. We had just a whole bunch of problems. We tried different things, and none of them worked."

Other sources speak of early harmonic vibration problems severe enough to shatter gearwheels. The final solution was to send power from the clutch to the transmission through an intermediate idler gear. That gave the powertrain four basic geared shafts—crank/clutch, idler, transmission mainshaft, and final drive—and meant that crankshaft rotation had to be reversed to make the rear wheels turn in the desired direction.

More second thoughts involved the alternator and shift linkage. The former was originally gear-driven from the output end of the crankshaft, but this was changed to a more conventional belt drive in the interest of reduced noise, which in turn dictated grouping the alternator with other ancillaries at the rear of the engine.

The linkage problem was far more complicated: how to transfer gearshift motion from the middle of the car all the way around to the back of the engine where the transmission was.

One early scheme employed a complex system of hydraulic lines. Wallace says this actually worked quite well—when it worked. Problems with heat and seals proved so annoying that the team scrapped the idea and evolved a straight mechanical linkage. Engine-block castings were changed to bring a tubular shifting rod straight through the crankcase from front to rear below the crankshaft; a system of cranks and rods then transferred motion up to the transverse gearshafts. The dauntingly elaborate, necessarily stiff-shifting mechanism that resulted is the single flaw in an otherwise brilliant powertrain.

Important detail revisions occurred in the body/chassis design. Let's start with the radiator. On the bare show chassis, it mounted in an odd lay-down position atop the front structure; this was later changed.

The first running car was the second step in the debugging process, and a

Though several cars were later converted there was only one real Miura Spider (*above*). The car was unveiled by Bertone at the 1968 Brussels motor show and was later rebuilt in zinc for an American metals company. Renamed the ZN 75, zinc was used in almost every possible location, and lead insulation was used in the doors and under the floor.

cooling problem surfaced quickly once Wallace got it out on the road. He remembers the solution mainly involved attention to radiator air-outlet ducting, but better airflow through the engine compartment was also needed.

Like the GT40, the original Miura body had a transparent exterior rear window—actually just a plastic sheet. Trouble was, it kept a lot of heat from escaping the engine compartment (and probably gathered a lot of oily dirt that quickly rendered it opaque). Adding vent holes provided only partial relief. Happily, replacing the window with a bank of open louvers provided the

The ZN 75 was a promotional piece and the maker's new zinc alloy, ILZRO 12, was used throughout the car. Unpainted, shiny zinc showed up everywhere on the exterior—the bumper, headlight surrounds, wheel arches, and hood. Even the engine, where carb stacks, manifolds, exhaust system, oil sump, and water pump housing were cast in zinc. The interior (*above*) was also chock-full of zinc replacement parts. Steering wheel, switches, instrument bezels, door handles, and handbrake lever received the treatment.

practical (though noisy) solution—and a distinctive styling feature that would later be imitated by other automakers and numerous accessory houses.

Of course, the Miura had a second rear window—in the bulkhead separating cockpit from engine compartment. With the engine just inches behind the cockpit, noise and heat levels in there would have been unbearable without the additional window. After an early trial with an elaborate double-walled, gas-filled glass pane, simpler construction in a special plastic called Visarm was found to provide adequate insulation.

Cockpit ventilation dictated another "aerodynamic" refinement. According to chronicler Chris Harvey, the first Miura had a small, driver-operable hatch in the roof at a point where low air pressure at speed would pull air out from inside. But it didn't work that well and ultimately gave way to a rank of small, fixed extractor vents like those on the original GT40.

Much less easily remedied was a cockpit that was simply too small. That's why the roofline was raised a little and the cabin lengthened beginning with Miura No. 3.

Some historians believe the cockpit was stretched to improve handling; others state that it was to make room for thicker heat and sound insulation in the firewall. Of the latter, Wallace says, "No, that was never changed. It was always inadequate! No, that [insula-

tion thickness] dimension never changed at all. It was just to get a little more room. The first two cars, the first two hand-built prototypes, were a little cramped. The additional length went into more foot room."

It amounted to 1.4 inches, leaving wheelbase on production Miuras at 97.5 inches. The height increase was much less—a mere 10 millimeters (about ⅜ inch)—but lowering the seats an equal amount.

All these improvements were built into operational car No. 3, the first Miura built to final production specs, though both the design and manufacturing details were further refined even after this. Aggravated by delays in gathering all needed components, the assembly line didn't really began to stir until late 1966. The first customer car finally went out the door early the next year—some 12 seemingly interminable months after Geneva.

The wait was worth it. Here's a sample of contemporary comment: "...one of the more memorable high points in the history of automotive architecture...furious performance and terrific roadholding...the most glamorous, exciting and prestigious sports car in the world...an absolute blast to drive on a winding road...a long surge of power and a beautiful noise that could best be described as ecstasy...this car is the ultimate."

So even after all those months, the Miura was still fresh and exciting, not

least because it was the only big mid-engine sports car on the market (for all the time that had passed, it wasn't enough for competitors to have issued replies). Even better, its radical design really worked, and Lamborghini could claim the fastest and most capable production car on earth.

It didn't escape Ferruccio Lamborghini that his most sensational car ran counter to the philosophy on which he had founded his automobile company. Lamborghini's goal was to manufacture premium cars with a standard of refinement that was higher than those of rival makers. He sought comfortable, quiet grand tourers without mechanical troubles. The Miura wasn't that sort of car at all, at least not in 1967. While it was undeniably splendid—fast, fun, and, if pushed hard, quite a challenge—it wasn't much of a tourer, and not a typical Lamborghini.

So the little firm deserves credit for making a serious attempt to improve the P 400, for though its initial flaws were many and obvious, sensational styling and thrilling performance virtually guaranteed that every Miura built would be sold. Wallace and Co. got right to work and ultimately made many refinements, probably more than on any other Lamborghini model. Some were put into production as soon they were ready. Others were part of two formal upgrades: the S-model, introduced in 1969, and the still-better SV that succeeded it two years later.

Incidentally, many of these modifications can be—and have been—made to early examples, P 400 owners apparently being less reluctant to individualize their cars this way than is usually the case with high-performance exotics. Of course, this tends to make model identification tricky, but that's more a problem for concourse judges and automotive historians.

The single greatest revision (so fundamental as to make retrofitting entirely impractical) was heavier-gauge sheet steel for the chassis. Effective with Miura No. 125, according to factory records, it brought metal thickness from 0.9-millimeter to an even 1.0 mm (0.039-inch). Dallara's original design calculations perhaps didn't fully anticipate the sheer ferocity of the final production car's performance, especially with the ever-grippier tires that became available after production commenced. As Bob Wallace admits, sensitive drivers could detect distinct chassis flex in hard work, and some early Miuras apparently suffered actual structural failure.

But Wallace notes that stouter steel wasn't the total cure, so various gussets were added at times for further structural strengthening, particularly where the front and rear extensions joined the central tub. These reinforcements can be retrofitted, and Wallace recommends just that. By the time production ended, both measures had rendered the chassis flex "very, very minimal," he says, though it was still noticeable if you were looking (and driving) hard enough.

Rear suspension was the second-most important area of change, and it was changed twice: for the S and again for the SV, each accompanied by upgraded tires. The former gained subtly altered mounting points that reduced squat under hard acceleration. The SV's suspension was completely redesigned in the front and rear, supplemented by much wider aft tires and rims that dictated bulging the rear fenders. Wallace says these revisions, together with the strengthened chassis, were enough to make the SV "pretty well completely a different car" compared to earlier Miuras. "The handling difference is an enormous improvement."

Wallace observes that two other problems were finally corrected with the SV. The solutions were linked. One

One interesting feature of the ZN 75 was the replacement of the rocker panel and rear wheel scoop with a zinc panel. Similar to that on a '66 Corvette, the gaudy trim panel disturbed the car's flowing lines. Careful inspection of an early drawing for the show car (*above*) reveals slightly different C-pillar scoops and uncovered engine.

was a new sump with sufficient added depth that the oil pickup no longer unported in hard cornering, thus eliminating the tendency of previous cars (most Miuras built, in fact) to bearing damage in sustained hard cornering.

Why didn't the factory correct this sooner? "They could have," Wallace allows, "but there was also a question of money. Lamborghini never wanted to throw anything away. There wasn't a great deal of money to change anything once things started going. Plus, the philosophy was, 'Oh, the customers will never drive that hard.' Which was bull, because they did."

The deeper sump coincided with the redesigned suspension to raise static rear ride height on the SV, and that plus a slight lowering at the front

altered its aerodynamic "angle of attack" so that the nose no longer lifted at very high speeds. Some earlier Miuras were fitted with various crude sheetmetal front spoilers toward the same end, but Wallace says none were effective.

Other interim improvements were less drastic but quite worthwhile. Vented brake rotors, an S running change, markedly reduced fade in severe use, and later SVs gained a partition between crankcase and transmission, thus providing separate oil supplies at last. The latter had the dual benefits of allowing lubricants suited to the specific needs of each mechanism, and of keeping contaminants generated by one from harming the other. The real reason for this belated change was to

The final and finest version of the Miura, the P 400 SV, was produced starting in 1971 (*above*). The single most important revision of the SV was the use of heaver gauge steel in chassis. Suspension and rear ride height was altered to combat lift, and a new oil sump was added.

provide for the equally belated installation of limited-slip differential (supplied by ZF), which couldn't work properly in the comparatively light engine oil of the previous shared sump. This may have contributed to an improvement in the shifting feel. Whereas some of the earlier Miuras had required a good deal of strength to get a gear, the SV's transmission mechanism had been massaged to the point where, while shifting effort was not exactly light, it was at least reasonable.

The Miura's brilliant 3.9-liter V-12 was also improved in stages. As ever, published horsepower figures are various and thus debatable (especially those in factory ads), but it's likely that the earliest Miuras packed no more than some 320 DIN horsepower at about 6500 rpm (though that was hardly chicken feed). Later P 400s seem to have had closer to the advertised 350 bhp at 7000 rpm.

For the S, reshaped combustion chambers, higher-lift cams and bigger carburetors on fatter manifolds brought output to 370 bhp at 7500 rpm (one source says 7700 rpm). The SV had the most Miura muscle—a claimed 385 bhp at 7850 rpm—thanks to still-different cam timing, bigger valves, and altered carbs. As this increased fuel consumption, Lamborghini offered a larger fuel tank (110 liters/29 U.S. gallons) as a new option. Of course, the SV's greater structural mass and wider tires pretty much negated its extra

power, so top speed wasn't up by much (if at all) compared to that of previous Miuras.

Running changes during the Miura's 5 ½ years of production also embraced numerous comfort and convenience details. Power windows ultimately ousted the original knuckle-scuffing manual window-winders to remove a source of real annoyance to many while making the Miura a little more like other Lamborghinis, and the two engine-cover latch handles gave way to one, a much handier arrangement. Beginning with the S, a locking glove box was installed, factory-fitted air conditioning and radio came at extra cost, and the original wood-rim steering wheel was exchanged for a leather-wrapped item. SVs added real leather interior trim, replacing the previous leather-look vinyl.

Other interim cabin changes involved passenger grab handles and, to comply with U.S. "secondary collision" rules, rocker switches to replace toggle types. For some reason, the original 200-mph speedometer on cars sent to non-metricated countries was later replaced by one calibrated to 190 mph.

There was no need to tamper much with the Miura's styling— and, wisely, Lamborghini didn't—but a few minor adjustments were made. The most visible involved the lay-back headlights, or rather the high-style grillework that initially surrounded them. On the earliest Miuras this took the form of black-

painted fins attached to the lights so that they, too, lifted up into the airstream—where they looked for all the world like eyelashes. The fins were soon separated to remain flush with the nose when the headlights were up. The SV arrived with no eyelashes at all, and it is these "plucked" headlights as well as the noticeably more muscular rear flanks that most easily identify this final Miura evolution.

Ascertaining correct production for any Lamborghini is often as difficult as pegging precise power numbers. The Miura is no exception. An exhaustive study by Pete Coltrin and Jean-Francois Marchet has put the total run at 762 units. Obviously, the factory's initial sales forecast for its wild new car was wildly off. Author Rob de la Rive Box breaks out the three versions as follows: 475 P 400s, 140 S-models, and 150 SVs. That makes 765 in all, three more than the Coltrin/Marchet total, but Box's P 400 figure undoubtedly includes the mockup show chassis and the two running prototypes. We hasten to add that other sources put SV volume at only 120.

The "last" Miura was built in late 1972 and wasn't delivered until the following January. We qualify "last" because a final, brand-new one was put together from leftover parts in 1975 to the order of Lamborghini fan Walter Wolf.

Every Miura but one was a coupe. The sole exception, not counting several cars later converted by individual owners, was an open-top proposal built by Bertone in 1968 and officially designated P 400 Roadster, though some Europeans insisted on calling it Spider. While it never had any form of top or side windows, numerous detail alterations to cockpit and rear body-work made it a serious study that attracted much favorable attention. But, as Bob Wallace says, there was no money for this or any other additional production model, and the Roadster was soon sold to the International Lead Zinc Research Organization. With Bertone's help, ILZRO turned it into the "Zn 75," a rolling exhibit of possible automotive applications for those metals.

Despite this, the Jota and several other conversion cars, the roadgoing production coupe was always the main focus of the factory's Miura business. However, the factory was going through one of its many financial crises at the time. After all, there was no commercial need whatsoever to enhance the image of the spectacular, sensual, and sensational P 400 that had so stunned the automotive world in 1966 and continues to draw eyes today.

In 1981, some eight years after the Miura had breathed its last, journalist Mel Nichols, who'd logged a lot of miles in the successor Countach but very few in a Miura, borrowed a privately owned SV for a get-acquainted gallop over remote British roads. Recalling the experience for *Automobile* magazine in 1986, he was surprised that this trend-setting machine "really felt nice and not as dated as I thought it would. I played a couple of times, taking second for some of the tighter bends and booting out really hard to see if the rear Pirellis would let go. They did, where current tires on today's good automobiles would not. The breakaway was lightning fast, too...."

As always, the engine was magnificent: "The rumble of sounds from the V-12 at tickover began to blend together on the way to that glorious midrange bellow. I was pushed back into the little race-like bucket. With less lifting of the nose and dipping of the tail than I expected, the SV rocketed ahead—hard, sharp, and truly potent, if not quite savage."

At steady speeds around 160 mph, Nichols found that the Miura "gave the impression of needing more road" than other cars of its type. The same was true when decelerating: "On the faster stretches, I found that the SV needed room to romp, weaving slightly under braking. And the brakes, good though they might have seemed a decade or two ago, were barely all right by today's standards. If you're playing with a Miura, play cautiously."

But play by all means: "The Miura was devastatingly fast for its time, and is still among the very quickest of cars, with the purpose and spirit of a sports-racer but produced for the road." Nichols then quoted a particularly fine bit of simile by another writer who had been just as bewitched by this magical motorcar. "He said, 'the Miura was the twentieth century's answer to the razor-taloned falcon, the favored suit of Swabian armor, the private bodyguard of Prussian mercenaries, a fine pair of dueling pistols, or any of the other virility symbols of bygone eras.'"

Though the interior was a carry-over, the engine was again revised to pump out 385 bhp at 7850 rpm. In addition, the crankcase and transmission now each had their own oil supply, which allowed for the instillation of a ZF limited-slip differential. While exterior changes were limited, headlight eyebrows were eliminated and the grille was widened.

Stefano Pasini records that *Il Cavaliere* himself saw the Miura as "a splendid paramour: very costly and unforgettable." How true this is, as the P 400 remains, above all else, an object of passion, a matter of purest emotion.

Automotive journalist Pete Lyons confessed that he, too, was unable to regard the Miura objectively. Of all cars, he said he holds the Miura to be one of the half-dozen most beautiful, exciting, and desirable. Lyons said that after spending two days with a Miura on late-'80s American roads, he found himself bemused by a mood of tristess, a bittersweet feeling that though something bright and beautiful had once danced across the world and was still visible, it had somehow been lost behind a hazy veil.

In setting down the experience for *Car and Driver*, he wrote: "Ah, but watch as the liquid light pours over her, so pretty it actually hurts. What sweet contrasts it reveals: her sensual, soft skin, her muscled wheels. *Contrappunti*! How lovely she is. How young."

model	1966-69 Miura P 400	1969-71 Miura P 400 S	1971-72 Miura P 400 SV
production	475	140	150
engine	dohc V-12	dohc V-12	dohc V-12
displacement cc/ci	3929/240	3929/240	3929/240
horsepower @ RPM (DIN)	350 @ 7000	370 @ 7700	385 @ 7850
torque @ RPM (lbs/ft)	280 @ 5500	286 @ 5500	286 @ 5000
length (mm/in.)	4370/170.4	4390/171.2	4390/171.2
width (mm/in.)	1760/68.6	1780/69.4	1780/69.4
height (mm/in.)	1050/41	1100/42.9	1100/42.9
wheelbase (mm/in.)	2500/97.5	2504/97.7	2505/97.7
track, front (mm/in.)	1400/54.6	1512/59	1410/55
track, rear (mm/in.)	1400/54.6	1512/59	1540/60
weight (kg/lbs)[1]	945/2079	1180/2596	1245/2739

[1]Factory dry-weight claims, actual numbers higher.

CHAPTER SIX

COUNTACH

AUTOMOTIVE DESIGN WAS

FOREVER CHANGED AT THE 1971

GENEVA MOTOR SHOW. ALONGSIDE

THE MIURA SV WAS THE LP 500,

A CAR THAT WOULD BECOME

THE SUPERCAR FOR THE

NEXT THREE DECADES.

In the early 1970s, Lamborghini faced a formidable challenge—finding a replacement for the stunning Miura. The resulting automobile was nothing short of unbelievable. At the 1971 Geneva motor show, the most refined version of the Miura ever produced, the SV, was simply opaqued by Lamborghini's new creation, the LP 500. Known internally as "Project 112," this car was so far ahead of its competitors that it would continue to be the class leader until being phased out in 1990.

A "gunslinger of a motor car," was the assessment of auto writer Pete Lyons. "This is a bad boy's car and everybody knows it," wrote *Car & Driver*'s Larry Griffin. If such metaphors seem too dark, too melodramatic, you have never seen or driven a Countach. In design and performance it eclipsed everything that had come before it.

It is an automobile that "treats velocity with the same casual contempt it does society," Lyons said. "In this car, a hundred miles in an hour is nothing. Such a rate is but an inadvertence, an abstract instant of position on a dial, an unnoticed gate through which one passes, effortlessly, into a realm where speed seems to have no taint of risk—and only barely of vice. It hardly seems to be moving at 60. At 120 it is as steady as an everyday car at 60. For the first time you feel 120 is not fast; it is merely twice 60. Your thoughts extrapolate: 180 would be merely half-again faster. This stupefying road machine, you well know, can easily reach 180, and at

that speed, you are quite sure, would leave the driver as utterly without qualm as it does at 90."

If the Miura made Lamborghini's name famous, the Countach made it immortal. It's no accident that both cars were conceived very much in the same spirit. Unlike other Lamborghinis, which had to be at least somewhat practical and civilized, the Countach had no purpose other than flat-out performance—a competition-inspired bullet train for two. At least that was the vision of those who designed and built it. To Ferruccio, it was merely the latest flagship of his fleet.

The Countach was primarily the brainchild of Paolo Stanzani, the assistant to Lamborghini's first chief engineer, Giampaolo Dallara, who'd taken over the job in 1968. It was under Stanzani and his assistant, methodical testing specialist Massimo Parenti, that the factory development team had refined Dallara's initially flawed Miura to near-perfection in the 1971 SV model. With that, their thoughts quickly turned to a still-better land-bound missile—an all-new car of Stanzani design.

There was no specific name at first, the effort being known simply as "Project 112." As Dallara had done with the Miura, Stanzani—with Bob Wallace right at his elbow, no doubt—began drawing on clean paper.

Despite the suspension improvements wrought for the SV, the rapid advances in the sciences of tires and high-speed dynamics were beginning to expose deficiencies in the basic

Miura chassis. Specifically, the team wanted to correct the high-speed front-end lift, the tendency to snap oversteer, the stiff gearshift action, and the excessive cockpit heat and noise.

Initial design and testing proceeded around an experimental tire that Pirelli had shown to Lamborghini, one that promised to give Sant'Agata's new supercar much higher cornering power than anything else on the road. But as Bob Wallace attests, "That tire was never released, [so] we had to put the Countach into production on some older Michelins, which weren't really right for it. In fact, they were terrible on the car. It took years before Pirelli came back with the P7, which was something like the tire the car had originally been designed to accept."

Since he was starting anew, Stanzani decided to rethink engine/transmission packaging, though a midships configuration would be retained. (Lamborghini could hardly abandon for the 1970s what it so thrillingly realized in the '60s.) What he devised was as fresh and imaginative and at least as elegantly practical as the Miura layout.

After putting the gearbox back on the end of the crankshaft, Stanzani turned the entire drivetrain 90 degrees so that it was longitudinal again—only *backward* from the usual orientation. This meant a "south-north" engine driving to a transmission mounted ahead of it; power then went back to the differential (still behind the engine) through a simple step-down gearset and a shaft running through a sealed

The LP 500 prototype (*left and below*) was designed by Marcello Gandini at Bertone. Underneath the car was a chassis of steel tubes, strengthened by steel plates. The car was fully operational and sported a powerful 4971 cc, 440 bhp V-12 engine. This engine did not live long however. During testing shortly after the car's debut, the engine caught fire. Luckily, the car was saved—only to be destroyed in crash testing.

tunnel in the sump under the bottom of the engine.

The in-sump driveshaft had two theoretical disadvantages: It forced the engine weight to be carried a few inches higher than in the Miura (thus raising the center of gravity), and it added a bit of overall weight.

Facing these disadvantages were numerous practical benefits. First, though drivetrain mass was higher, it was also further forward than in the Miura. This offered the possibility of putting more of the Countach's total weight on its front wheels. This would counteract both the nose-lift and tail-snap tendencies (though aerodynamics and suspension geometry would also enter the equation). In fact, production Countachs, which were heavier than the prototype concept, had almost exactly the same 42/58 percent front/rear weight distribution as the Miura.

Second, the forward clutch mounting left the differential and rear-wheel centerline as close behind the engine as they could be, so the engine occupied the minimum possible amount of the wheelbase (short of placing it *over* the axle line, as Ferrari did in its Berlinetta Boxer).

Third, the reversed inline drivetrain put the gearlever right under the driver's hand for improved shift action—aided by a switch from Porsche synchronizers to a lower-effort ZF system. Finally, much less of the engine's bulk was close to the cockpit, so insulation was easier. Granted, the hot transmission now sat between driver and passenger, but that was the case in most any sports car and easy enough to handle.

Of course, in situating the long V-12 lengthwise, Stanzani was abandoning one of the chief benefits of the Miura's transverse layout: its wide, unencumbered footwells. In the new car, driver and passenger sat between wide sills, each containing a fuel tank, and had to cram their feet into comparatively

Several other prototypes were made up in the Countach's two-year gestation period. This car (*left*) already had the roof-mounted periscope deleted, NACA ducts cut into the rear flanks, and hoods over the C-pillar scoops installed as on the production model. The most visually impacting feature of the Countach is most certainly the scissor-wing doors (*below left*). Although in real life its tough just to get over the sheer lowness of the car, just 41.7 inches.

sheetmetal stiffeners welded together with a handmade steel bodyshell. Production models would delete the sheet and have a more elaborate structure welded up from round tubes, as well as a non-stressed aluminum body.

Though a slow and costly type of chassis to fabricate, the space frame was adopted partly because Lamborghini again did not plan on building many examples of its new supercar, and partly because welded-tube construction was relatively easy for a low-volume builder. But where the Miura chassis suffered persistent stiffness problems, the final Countach design was enormously strong. Wallace also notes that corrosion had proven a significant problem with the Miura tub; a tubular frame was considered easier to rust-proof.

Another major difference was engine displacement, which in the Countach prototype was 25 percent greater than in the Miura. The now-familiar 3929 cubic-centimeter (239.7 cubic-inch) quad-cam V-12 was treated to a Detroit-style bore-and-stroke job, ending up at 4971 cc (303.35 cid) on bore stretched from 82 to 85 mm (3.23 to 3.35 inches) and stroke extended from 62 to 73 mm (2.44 to 2.87 inches). According to Wallace, the basic block casting couldn't be stretched this far without some makeshift steel spacers, but it was just an experiment anyway. The result was a factory-claimed 440 DIN horsepower at 7400 rpm and 366 pounds/feet of torque peaking at 5000 rpm. These were substantial improvements over the 3.9's outputs and just the sort of muscle expected in the world's ultimate road car.

This 5.0-liter engine, located longitudinally but still *posterior*, gave Project 112 its official designation: LP 500. To differentiate it from the Miura (which was then still in production), the P 400 became known as the TP 400, the "T" for *trasversale* ("transverse").

narrow, angled tunnels between the front wheels. This was unfortunate, though it's hard to imagine many sales being lost just because seating in this new ultracar was more like that of a race car. Lamborghini salespeople could always answer any such objections by pointing out that wheelbase was a mere 95.5 inches, two inches

shorter than the Miura's and almost identical to that of the first-ever Lamborghini, the 350 GTV.

Stanzani departed from Miura practice in most every other area of the Countach design. For example, instead of being of all sheet-steel construction, the prototype chassis was a space-frame of square-section steel tubes and

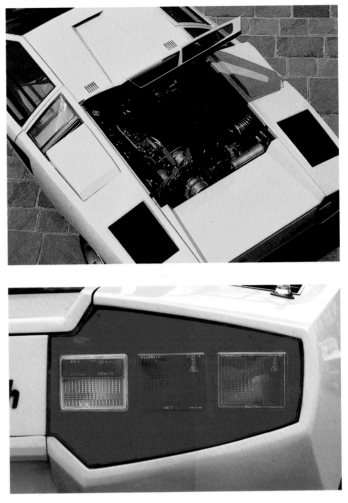

For styling, Lamborghini turned once more to Bertone's talented Marcello Gandini. He did not disappoint, rendering another breakthrough design. Though obviously inspired by contemporary GT endurance racers, such as the Porsche 917, as well as by Bertone's own 1968 Carabo ("Beetle"), Gandini's Countach was like no other road car in history. It fearlessly took up the wedge profile that was becoming *de rigueur* for competition cars in those early days of downforce aerodynamics, tempered by one of the geometric forms with which Gandini was experimenting at time—not the hexagon, as on the Marzal, but the trapezoid. The result was much less sensuous than the Miura, yet graceful in its way, and the maestro managed to retain enough animal curvature to give the LP 500 an agile look.

By now, some five years after working on the Miura, Gandini was obviously quite comfortable with the fundamentally different proportions dictated by mid-engine positioning,

and the sketches that multiplied on his drawing board no longer contained the long-hood found on his earlier cars. Indeed, the LP 500 emerged with practically no hood at all. Instead, an expansive, steeply sloped windshield plunged almost straight forward into a knife-edge nose with little apparent break at the windshield base. A small hinged nose panel flipped up to reveal the spare tire and a few ancillaries. From the windshield back was a pronounced "mound" profile appropriate for the huge engine lurking within. Bold vertical slats were cut in behind the doors to feed a high, sidemount radiator on each side.

The LP 500 body was just as startling and dramatic everywhere else. The near-horizontal "tunnelback" roof made scant concession to rearward vision, so a central rear-facing periscope was faired-in on top just aft of the windshield crown. As on the "beetle-winged" Carabo, there were long doors hinged to lift straight up in modified gullwing style. Roll-down

Despite the fact that it was over two years between prototype and production, the engine (*top*) of the LP 400 was a carryover V-12 with a displacement 3929 cc. However, this engine was placed in a south-north configuration just above the rear wheels. The transmission then ran forward between the front seats. Power was the routed back through the entire length of the crankcase to the differential. It was a very-space efficient package and aided in weight distribution, but it raised the roll center and tended to overheat.

windows were precluded by the marked difference in curvature between the greenhouse and bodysides, but a separate opening "windowlette" was provided for ventilation as well as access to tollbooths and the like. Engine access was via a front-hinged lid immediately aft of the cockpit. Behind that was a second panel covering a small trunk. Retracting headlights were incorporated near the tops of the front fenders; immediately below were recessed parking/turn-signal lights styled to look like faired-in headlights. Asymmetric rear wheel arches were another daring departure from conventionality.

Lifting the doors (a sight in itself) revealed a similarly unusual two-place cockpit—very clean and futuristic—dominated by a high center tunnel bearing a hefty, resolutely vertical gear lever. Digital instruments, a new and highly experimental development in the early '70s, were employed on the prototype. The same go-for-broke approach was seen in the extensive (and expensive) use of magnesium castings for components like suspension uprights, steering rack, engine mounts, oil-system housings and sump—but not the engine block itself.

Inevitably, it took a last-minute rush to get the LP 500 finished in time for its world premiere at the 1971 Geneva show. Reportedly, it was very late on the night work was being completed at Bertone's Grugliasco plant—perhaps even as the menacing wedge slinked out of the paint booth in its bright lemon yellow—that someone stood back, took a look, and exclaimed, *"Countach!"*

"COON-tahsh" or "CUN-touch" (Italians use both pronunciations) is an expression in the local Piemontese dialect that seems difficult to render in English without offending someone. Even the hard-bitten Bob Wallace squirms and comes close to blushing when asked to explain it: "Aw, well, it can mean one of about ten different things. It depends on how it's used more than anything else. It, uh, can be an obscenity or it can be sort of, 'Oh, you wondrous, sensuous thing,' or, ah...." Let us relieve the good Mr. Wallace from his discomfiture by say-

ing that *"Countach!"* is the sort of thing a northern Italian male might utter to express appreciation for a particularly attractive female.

As noted, the Countach, like the Miura before it, was envisioned as a *very* limited edition—not so much a money-maker as a low-volume showcase for the manufacturer's technical and artistic prowess, with little regard for practicality and price. Again, however, the public had other ideas, and it's likely that the first offers to buy came within minutes of the Geneva show's opening. But like the Miura that wowed the crowds in early '66, the Countach of early 1971 was nowhere near ready for sale.

That first yellow car was just a prototype, little more than a hasty mockup, though it was fully roadworthy. With a laugh, Wallace quashes the often-repeated story that he drove it straight from the Bertone plant to Geneva over the Alps in winter. "Naw, it was about 2 a.m. We sent it up there by truck!" In

fact, almost every detail of the LP 500 needed substantial revision before Lamborghini could think of beginning even limited production.

First of all, the big-bore engine blew up almost immediately. The car was saved from complete immolation, but the 5.0-liter was never replaced. All subsequent testing was done with a 3.9 motor, although the LP 500 type designation was left unchanged.

Paralleling the Miura experience, overheating surfaced as the next immediate problem. Even the 3.9 furnace within the belly of the beast was too

With all of the doors and hatches open the Countach looked like a vehicle from another planet (*above*). Inside the cabin (*far left*) was noisy, hot, and cramped; but for the experienced driver, there was no better place to be. In the right hands the LP 400 could get from 0-60 mph in 5.6 seconds and reach a top speed of 179 mph.

much for the twin sidemount radiators buried in its flanks. Extensive revisions brought about a completely changed cooling system. Retained were the side radiators, but the louvers had to be exchanged for a pair of grotesque scoops atop the rear fenders. Also, NACA inlets were added behind the doors.

Another problem was also aerodynamic in nature. In their zeal to avoid the well-known nose-lift tendency of early Miuras, Lamborghini and Bertone gave the LP 500 a very wedgy front that proved *too* effective.

"There was excessive downforce on the nose of the first car," Wallace reports. "Under weight transfer under braking, the car was a little scary." And you can imagine how much tail-wobble a car must have for the likes of Bob Wallace to call it "scary." In any case, it was cured by reducing the nose slope—actually by raising the "bumper point" a little—a change first seen on the last of the three Countach prototypes built before production began.

On the subject of aerodynamic instability, some critics have claimed that aft body shaping disposes the Coun-

Though the body of the original prototype LP 500 was made of steel, the production body panels were rendered in aluminum (*top*). Also the door windows were split in two with only the bottom half lowering, making visibility even worse. In 1982 an updated Countach appeared—the LP 5000 S (*bottom*). Engine displacement was up to 4754. Horsepower was unchanged but torque was up by 20 pounds/feet. Underneath the skin, the suspension was reworked and an emissions-satisfying air pump was added.

Walter Wolf, a Canadian businessman with aspirations of ownership, talked Lamborghini into building several specials for him. In addition to the Miura SV he had built from spare parts several years after production was halted, he had three Countachs built to his design. One sported a unique rear wing, fatter Pirelli P7 tires, and a larger engine. All of these features were added to the LP 5000 S when it arrived in 1982. Some rear wings (*right*) were electronically adjustable from inside the cabin.

to Sicily the following week to view the classic Targa Florio open-road race. By the time they returned to Sant'Agata, they knew they had a real car. It was at this point that Lamborghini decided to proceed with production.

Two more Countach prototypes were built, both key steps toward the ultimate production design. Because the 5.0-liter engine had proven unreliable, the trusty 3.9 was standardized and the model designation switched to LP 400.

Onto the all-new, all-tube chassis was hung an all-new suspension built with the steel tubes of a pure race car to substitute for the modified production-car pressings of the LP 500 prototype. That car had used metal-to-metal suspension pivots, however, and they made things just too harsh and noisy. Instead of reverting to conventional rubber bushings, as on the Miura, the development team adopted nylon pivots to give the production Countach the best of both worlds.

As they were working on what was still intended to be the world's ultimate exotic, they chose to craft the bodyshell of aluminum a scant 1 mm thick. They also specified light-but-strong and very costly Belgian-made glass for windshield and side windows, used even more magnesium throughout, and added expensive racing-type Koni shocks and Girling disc brakes all-round. But the digital gauges and periscope were abandoned as impractical, and there were numerous detail changes inside and out. A proper windshield wiper system was added (like many prototypes, the LP 500 didn't have one, until Wallace himself installed a single blade so he could drive it).

Painted a hot red, the first LP 400 appeared at Geneva '72. The day the show closed, Wallace took it over for a second round of hard road and track testing. Lessons learned there were applied to prototype No. 3, which had the aforementioned modified nose. This car, painted green, appeared at Paris in '73. Meanwhile, the short, hard life of the yellow No. 1 car ended with a barrier crash-test at the Motor Industry Research Association in England.

The first time Wallace sat in the red prototype was when he picked it up for the drive home after Geneva '72. He remembers its seating position was completely different from No. 1's:

tach to *rear* lift. Wallace denies this, and snorts his derision at the optional inverted rear airfoil that was adopted after he left the firm: "I think all the wing on the car does is make it look racy and slow it down. There were no real tests done on the efficiency of the wing on the car. It was just tacked on."

Despite that initial instability under hard braking, Wallace was agreeably surprised by the good behavior of the yellow LP 500. Right away, he says, he could feel that even this raw prototype was a better machine than the finely

honed Miura SV: "The car was very, very quick, and far more stable than the Miura was. It had substantially more wheel travel on bump and rebound.... And due to its suspension geometry, it was a far more stable, far more forgiving car, a far superior handling car right from the start."

In mid-May 1972, Wallace took this very first Countach to Monaco for the same kind of public airing the first Miura prototype had enjoyed six years earlier. It proved so fast, competent, and reliable that he and Stanzani ran it down

"Stylists are smaller than normal people," he remarks with a wry smile. "Or they think of things as being smaller. When I first got that first tubular prototype chassis, the red one, my knees were level with my eyes...." He even had to throw out the oh-so-stylish multi-block upholstery in favor of "just a padded sheet of aluminum" so he could fit.

Such matters would ultimately be fixed on production cars, of course. Meanwhile, Wallace set off across southern Europe on long days of high-speed testing. He found No. 2 excellent for that kind of driving and raves about its performance to this day. (Indeed, he keeps a photo of it in a place of honor behind his desk in Phoenix.)

At last, the Countach was ready for production—albeit very limited production. Successful though it was, the Miura had opened a commercial can of worms by being too much car for too many of its buyers. Accordingly, the initial plan was to restrict the Countach to those who could prove them-

selves not just keen but capable, skilled drivers who really knew what to do with an ultra-fast road car that acted more like a racer. Poseurs need not apply. In fact, Lamborghini was reluctant to offer air conditioning not only because it sapped performance but because it might render the car just civilized enough for such pretenders. This decision would be overturned once the company changed hands, but in the beginning, the Countach had a soul as pure as that of any Le Mans racer.

The times were changing and the tide of events seemed against the Countach. It had taken the little development team three long years to make a saleable product of it—three long, difficult years that saw the rise in labor unrest that hastened the decline of *Cavaliere* Lamborghini's fortunes. By the time the first production LP 400 bravely greeted its public at the 1974 Geneva show, Ferruccio had sold out to Swiss partners Georges-Henri Rossetti and Rene Leimer. For *Automobili Ferruccio Lamborghini SpA*, the future did not look bright.

First seen on the Bravo show car by Bertone in 1974, the distinctive five-hole Lamborghini wheels (*above*) were fitted on all Countachs from the LP 400 S on. Distinctive fiberglass wheel arches were added on the 400 S to accommodate updated tire technology.

That makes the automotive community's reaction to the first production Countachs even more remarkable. Remember, the Countach had become somewhat of a familiar face between the debut of its prototype in 1971 and the launch of the roadgoing model in mid-1974. But it was such an alien face, one still so clearly from some distant future, that it mesmerized even the most jaded observers, especially motor journalists, for writer after writer was moved to measure the car by its impact on non-enthusiasts.

"The people who live in the outskirts of Modena are used to seeing exotic cars 'on test,'" said Ray Hutton in Britain's *Autocar*. "But this one still makes them stop in their tracks, stare, smile and wave in encouragement." *Road & Track*'s Tom Bryant concluded

During the 1980s the Countach became a rare commodity in the United States. Ever tightening emissions regulations and safety standards made the car impossible to modify to meet requirements. Finally Lamborghini began to sell a U.S. specific model with fuel injection. Up until then, U.S. citizens had to live with gray market modifications like unsightly front bumpers (*left*) and seriously detuned engines.

that the evocative name was appropriate, "as the Countach inspires exclamations from nearly everyone who sees it. It is the first sports car I've driven that brought older ladies out of campers to look it over while parked at a coffee shop."

Doug Blain told readers of Britain's *CAR* magazine that "in town, the Countach creates as much of a sensation as would a full-blown Can Am Porsche or any other racing car...." Out in the country, the "science-fiction silhouette proved more effective than anything I have yet known at shifting even the more tenacious Topolinos from the fast lane.... The Countach breathes naked aggression from every pore: just to look at it is either to want

to climb in and thrash the living daylights out of it, or else to run."

Mel Nichols opined in Australia's *Sports Car World* that "if the success of a car's styling is measured by the attention it gets and the effect it has on people, then the Countach ranks supreme. It is an outlandish vehicle, almost unreal. Seeing it stark and alone on a deserted road made you feel as if you'd been transported to another time and another planet."

Outlandish and unreal: That was how almost everyone viewed the Countach. As an expression of the stylist's art, Lamborghini's new supercar was a triumph. Yet oddly enough, that far-out styling did an injustice to the car beneath it. On the road, the

LP 400 was brilliant in a way its coachwork was not.

Though undeniably dramatic, Marcello Gandini's body design made for a very awkward, even unpleasant automobile to live with. Take the large "scissor-wing" doors. They pivoted up and well forward, but were nonetheless clumsy despite assistance from gas-filled struts. Adding to the problem were excessively wide door sills. Once seated, occupants usually felt as if they'd entered a race car—which in a sense they had, because things were just as snug here.

Straight ahead, where the bodywork all but vanished, your view was excellent; in any other direction there seemed to be nothing *but* bodywork.

Even the right door mirror was cunningly located so the A-pillar blocked most of it.

Owing to the sharp upper-body tumblehome, each door window was split in two (three counting the fixed front ventpanes): a non-opening upper and a drop-down lower, separated by a horizontal bar. Trouble was, the lower part was too small for sticking one's head through for a look-see when backing up. The rear-quarter windows should have helped, but didn't: too small, laid almost flat, just perfect for viewing the radiator scoops. The only safe way to reverse a Countach was to open the door, sit on the sill and look back over the roof while somehow manipulating the pedals.

The "scissor-wing" doors may have been a great idea, however badly driven Countachs sometimes wound

Finally in 1985 the LP 5000 QV (*Quattrovalvole*) was ready. This car featured an all new engine, revised front and rear suspensions, better cooling, and an effective air conditioning system (*above* and *below*). The big news had to be the engine. Still based on the Bizzarrini design of 1963 it now sported four-valve heads and increased displacement. Horsepower was up to 420 at 7000 rpm.

One change to the Countach that was less well received was the new front and rear bumpers. Because the frame of the car was never designed to accept integrated bumpers, large black rubber ones had to be tacked on (*right*). Front and rear lines were destroyed, but at least the Countach was back in the U.S. All vertical body panels were made of heavier gauge aluminum, which added weight, but made the care less prone to costly dings and dents.

up on their roofs. A steel roll cage provided sturdy support in that event, but occupants quickly found out that it was quite difficult to evacuate from an inverted Countach. This problem was recognized from the start, and there was much talk of using a kick-out windshield and even explosive emergency bolts in the door hinges. Neither idea was adopted, though. To this day many people believe Countachs had special pull-out "lynch pins." While this perfectly good idea has been applied to certain aircraft, this Lamborghini legend is another of the false ones. Prudent Countach drivers simply strive to keep the rubber side down.

These and other design irritations made the Countach wildly impractical for everyday use, which raises the question of why the Countach has always been such a huge hit with the public.

"As a roadgoing automobile, the Lamborghini Countach is absolutely useless for anything a citizen of America is allowed to do," wrote Pete Lyons. "It's guaranteed, therefore, to bring lust swelling up in your heart. It's the sort of object you long to possess for all the wrong reasons. It's a seven-year-itch car, an illicit weekend in Lugano...sort of car."

Yet when doing what it was built to do, the immense competence of the thing banishes all thoughts of everyday absurdities. The Countach is surely one of the greatest pure-performance road cars ever to carve a corner or attack an *autostrada*. Driven the way Paolo Stanzani and Bob Wallace intended—hard and sharp, with spirit but with feeling—it is a marvelous ride, perhaps the most exciting one outside a race course.

Like so many great performers, the Countach demanded certain skills from those who master it. Not the least of these was decisiveness. Said *R&T*'s

Bryant: "It became apparent quickly that this was not a fragile car to be treated with teacup-and-watercress-sandwich fingers, but a sturdy, high-performance machine that needs a touch of muscle and an aggressive attitude."

Given that, the Countach would reward you with what Blain termed "perfection in performance and behavior [that] brings fast driving to the level of squash or fencing as an exhilarating and highly exacting but at the same time rather exhausting activity." Exhausting? Yes, if the car was used to its limits. "To be effective, you must get in there and boss the thing, using muscle but not force, urging it deeper and deeper into corners with little twitches of the wheel, banging the gears home, stamping on brake and clutch till you ache all over."

But that's where the workout ended. Nichols observed that the "suspension is set hard so that [the car] rides very firmly around town. Yet...it is not uncomfortable, merely reassuring. At speeds in bends this stiffness means

Along with a deeper chin spoiler the rear wing continued as an option on the 5000 QV (*top* and *right*). Inside, the car was mostly a carryover from previous editions, but some switchgear was replaced and padding was added around the center console. It's easy to spot Americanized versions of the Countach by the two humps on the rear engine cover (*right*). European models have just one hump in the center to clear the six centrally located Weber carburetors.

that the car stays extraordinarily flat. It snaps around curves like an electric slot racer, answering the steering with lightning quick response and precision and displaying a honed sharpness....There is never any understeer, and only oversteer when you want it with power." Summing up the enormous satisfaction of Countach driving, Nichols said the car merely "feels so purposeful, making you drive with an easy precision and a clear, relaxed mind."

It's inevitable with cars like this that someone will ask, "what will she do?" With the Countach, nobody really knows. Yes, a good many test numbers have been printed over the years, but they've always seemed to be qualified by circumstances: mechanical problems, lack of a suitable test venue, sometimes both. The plain fact is, the Countach has generally been faster than most available roads.

The original 3.9-liter Countach V-12 was supposed to belt out 375 horse-

power at 8000 rpm. That was 10 bhp less than the output quoted for the Miura SV, a difference that's been blamed partly on the use of sidedraft rather than vertical carburetors, though the Countach's were larger. Against that, the Countach was aerodynamically steadier at high speed than the Miura, and made it easier to hold the throttle longer.

Hutton reported that Wallace had once observed 290 km/h—180.2 mph—at 7600 rpm in the green No. 2 prototype on a timed 5 kilometer stretch of Fiat's private superhighway. Given a few more clicks, Bob thought he could have reached 7800 rpm and an even 300 km/h—186.4 mph. Wallace later told Nichols that he saw 297 km/h—a tad under 185 mph (presumably in a production car)—and that "there was a little more to come."

Acceleration is similarly problematic. In testing their first Countach, *Road & Track*'s crew clocked 0-60 mph in 6.8 seconds and the quarter-mile in 14.4

At the rear, large bumperettes and a new rear panel were added—all in the interest of safety (*top*). The view out the rear window was cut down even further by the raised engine cover and the optional rear wing. But, with so much horsepower at hand, who cared what was behind you!

It is easy to tell the differences between the U.S. spec and European spec models. The U.S. model has the large front bumper (*top*), and the European model had the older-style rear fascia, one humped engine cover, and no bumperette (*left*).

seconds at 105.5 mph, but confessed that their privately owned loaner had been babied. Then they added that colleagues at Britain's *Motor*, "by suppressing their feelings of mechanical sympathy" and dumping the clutch at 7000 rpm, got 5.6 seconds to 60, 14.1 seconds in the quarter and "two black lines 50 yards long." Perhaps we should simply state that Countach acceleration was more than adequate from the start.

Like other Lamborghinis, the Countach arrived with a lot of development potential, though it would take time to be fully realized. Yet even as the first customer cars were being delivered, the desire was stirring within Lamborghini to make the Countach better. One of those with the strongest desire was one of the first customers.

By some accounts, Walter Wolf purchased production Countach No. 1, having taken delivery as soon after Geneva '74 as the factory would release a car to him. A Canadian of Austrian birth, Wolf was not unlike Ferruccio Lamborghini himself: a burly, life-loving entrepreneur who enjoyed getting what he wanted and had the means to do it. He had a strong presence in the oil industry and was thus able to indulge his passion for auto racing by forming his own team (Jody Scheckter drove for Walter Wolf Racing in Formula 1 during '77 and '78 before becoming World Champion in '79). Reflecting his interest in *Automobili Ferruccio Lamborghini SpA*, Wolf even considered buying the firm from its Swiss owners of that period, Georges-Henri Rossetti and Rene Leimer.

Before that, Wolf's involvement with Lamborghini affairs was as a very enthusiastic customer who wasn't always content with the factory issue. He thus somehow talked the engine shop into building him a 5.0-liter V-12

like the one Wallace had blown up in 1971, and had it installed in his first Countach. When he sold that car, Wolf had the engine transplanted into a new Countach, done up in his competition livery (deep blue with gold pinstripes) and sporting a prominent racing-style wing atop the rear deck. The same engine later went into a third Wolf Countach. It's likely that this big-bore experience, rather more rewarding the second time around, helped give Lamborghini the confidence to go ahead with a similar production engine a few years later.

Wolf was definitely behind the adoption of Pirelli's low-profile high-tech P7 tire for the evolutionary LP 400 S of 1978. He'd already had one of his own cars altered to suit the wider, grippier rubber, and it worked so well that he insisted the factory look into it. "It's true," says Wallace, for once not cutting down a favorite Lamborghini fable. "Wolf paid for Dallara to come back and work out the revised suspension geometry, and also for all the testing they did up on Fiat's freeway."

To accommodate the squat tires, rather graceless fiberglass fender flares were tacked on, the front ones con-

nected by an aggressive chin spoiler—all of which succeeded in making the S look even more menacing than earlier Countachs. Wheels were also changed, again following Wolf's example, the relatively plain original rims giving way to a much bolder (and suitably wider) five-hole "telephone dial" type (as first seen on Bertone's Urraco-based 1974 Bravo show car).

Lamborghini finally got around to a "five-liter" production engine in 1982. It was initially offered as an option, perhaps with the hope of using up existing 3.9 stores. So equipped, the car was officially designated LP 500 S, same as the original Countach prototype of 11 years before, though some later examples were badged "5000 S" on the tail.

The new engine wasn't quite the same as the original 5.0-liter. Designed to meet ever-tightening emissions regulations, it differed in displacement (4754 cc/290 cid), bore and stroke dimensions (85.5×69 mm/3.37×2.72 inches), and in having lower, 9.2:1 compression. It thus claimed only 375

DIN horsepower, same as the 3.9, but achieved it at a more relaxed 7000 rpm.

Highlighting the Countach's third major revision, announced in March 1985, was four-valve cylinder-head architecture, by then almost universal in racing and spreading rapidly among the better road cars. Engineers also stretched stroke to 75 mm (2.95 inches) to bring total capacity up to 5167 cc (315 cid), tightened compression to 9.5:1, and reinstated downdraft Weber carburetors. In European tune, DIN horsepower climbed to a healthy 455, again peaking at 7000 rpm. The car was rebadged LP 5000 QV *Quattrovalvole* ("four-valve," 48 in all on this V-12).

A number of other alterations—some good, some not so good—occurred along with and in between these model changes. For example, there were useful periodic detail revisions to suspension and brakes—and patchwork solutions to U.S. safety standards (most depressingly, the blocky bumpers slapped on in the 1980s by the U.S. importer, then by Sant'Agata itself). Equipment was

gradually upgraded, too; even air conditioning was usually installed.

While all this fiddling evolved a more civilized Countach, it was also made for a larger and heavier Countach. "They raised the body on the frame, and also cut and welded bits and pieces into the body," groans Bob Wallace, who with some disgust has seen his original compact, super-light supercar put on as much fat as muscle over the years.

"And all the original magnesium is gone now," he adds. "It was good on a pure performance vehicle, if the owner would look after it properly, but it's just impractical in everyday service. It corrodes too easily. You can't expect most owners to wash down the underside of the car in the winter. People keep driving it in the snow...."

So even after 15 years, the Countach still had plenty of flaws—perhaps too many for The Ultimate Exotic. Yet it's fair to say that the efforts lavished on it by Wallace, his colleagues, and their successors are some reasons Lamborghini still exists as an automaker. Despite an impractical design, rampant inflation, and a painfully slow production pace, unflagging demand for this model is what kept Lamborghini from teetering into the abyss during its long period of economic darkness and labor union enmity in the Seventies. In short, the Countach single-handedly saved Lamborghini. The Urraco, Silhouette, and Jalpa couldn't do it; nor could the Cheetah, and certainly not the BMW and Fiat contracts undertaken in those desperate years.

That Lamborghini has survived is nothing short of miraculous, except that its founding spirit still burns bright. Even today, visitors to the now-faded Sant'Agata factory depart amazed that the firm's original commitment to building the finest roadgoing sports cars imaginable is as strong as it ever was.

The exquisite *Quattrovalvole* engine, a much-altered V-12 but still a direct descendant of Giotto Bizzarrini's 1963 original, played a big part in Lamborghini's resurgence, especially in America. When the Countach was first schemed, the factory didn't intend to bother with modifications for the special requirements of the U.S. Americans would have to dream from afar. Of course, Americans wanted this spectacular flyer as much as anyone, even though a car capable of three-mile-a-minute velocities made no sense whatsoever in a land with a blanket 55-mph speed limit.

Nevertheless, Lamborghini responded directly for a time, selling a few Countachs under an exemption from federal safety and emissions standards for low-volume producers. When that special dispensation ran out, various independent shops—part of the so-called gray market—stepped in to "federalize" individual cars for wealthy individuals who would not be denied. Washington eventually cracked down on this, too. By then, however, there were new owners in Sant'Agata more willing and able than prior regimes to tackle the problems of compliance.

Americans unwilling to truck with the gray market missed out on the Countach from the mid-1970s through about 1982. Then came Jasjit Rarewala, proprietor of California-based Lamborghini Cars of North America, who decided to make the Countach fully U.S.-legal and asked Sant'Agata for help, which he received. By the time the QV engine was ready, the success of Rarewala's interim conversion

efforts—plus an upturn in Lamborghini's fortunes—had prompted the factory to build a federal version entirely in Italy.

The result was a 1986 U.S.-spec 5000 QV with bumpers and specially engineered Bosch KE-Jetronic fuel injection to satisfy the respective demands of the DOT and EPA. SAE net horsepower was a rousing 420—less than eight percent below the output of the European engine—over a broad 7000-7500-rpm range. Torque was equally impressive: 340 pounds/feet at 5000 rpm.

In the November 1986 issue of *Automobile*, the peripatetic Mel Nichols stated that this federal QV had run 0-60 mph in "a shade over" five seconds, 0-100 mph in 10.8 and the quarter-mile in precisely 13 seconds in the hands of factory testers. Still, it took a trip to Italy's high-speed Nardo test track to confirm that even a "clean"

Countach could reach upwards of 180 mph. Comparing the *Quattrovalvole* to the 1982 American-spec S-model, *Road & Track* reported 0-60 at 5.2 seconds (versus 5.7) but saw "only" 173 mph flat out (versus 150 before).

There was more good news, as Nichols relayed in the aforementioned *Automobile* piece: "Like the '87 European Countach, the new U.S. model is a better car than the early four-valves in other ways.... Chief experimental

In April of 1987, Chrysler took control of *Automobile Lamborghini SpA*, and infused a great deal of cash and technology. Most of this new power did not surface until the Diablo in 1990, however in 1988 Lamborghini released a Countach model to celebrate the company's 25th anniversary. Though this 25th Anniversary Countach (*below*) was mostly a cosmetic model, the revised exterior took some of the rough edges from the original design and increased aerodynamics.

engineer Massimo Ceccarani says proudly, 'We've made the Countach better throughout and not just developed the new U.S. engine.' To improve steering response and stability, he's tweaked the front suspension geometry, moved the location of the steering rack, and changed the rate of the rear springs. The oil and water cooling is better, the air conditioning is more effective, and the build quality is finer."

While they were sorting out the *Quattrovalvole*, Lamborghini engineers also were working on what came to be known as a "super Countach." A test bed for future technology, the car had some composite exterior body panels and also ran four-wheel drive.

It was a pleasant surprise in September 1988 when Lamborghini celebrated its 25th year as an automaker with a special Anniversary Edition Countach. It was even more pleasing when the car was not just a cosmetically enhanced Countach and emerged instead as probably the finest all-around Countach ever.

Most obvious was substantially new exterior styling—the most sweeping change in the car's look since its introduction. Straked air intakes appeared on the lower body in front of the wheel arches. New panels over the engine compartment and rear fenders were highlighted by gracefully integrated radiator grille units that replaced the tacked-on-looking scoops. Besides softening the Countach's lines, the new ducting increased airflow through the engine bay and, along with a larger radiator fan and a beefed up water pump, cured the Countach of its propensity to overheat in traffic. The

panels that formed these intakes, plus the new front fender surrounds, trunk lid, and engine cover, were made from composite materials pioneered on the super Countach. They were lighter than the previous aluminum components. And since they were molded, they could be manufactured to finer tolerances than the hand-formed aluminum pieces.

The Anniversary Edition's engine was unaltered from its *Quattrovalvole* specification; Lamborghini apparently didn't want to risk having to recertify the V-12 for certain markets. The European version retained its sextet of Weber two-barrel carburetors, while the U.S. variant used Bosch K-Jetronic fuel injection. Both versions now had some of their accessories attached before the engine was installed, however, so reliability was theoretically improved. The engine bay was substantially cleaned up, with wires and hoses rearranged for a tidier look and easier servicing.

U.S. safety regulations were quite evident on the nose of the 25th Anniversary car, where the unsightly front rubber bumper blocks were retained for the American market. A

new composite tail panel, however, met Federal crash standards without modification. Complementing the suspension and steering revisions given the '88 model were the Anniversary Countach's new Pirelli P Zero tires with their asymmetrical tread design and use of two rubber compounds across their width. The size remained at 225/50ZR15 in front and 345/35ZR15 in back, but new two-piece aluminum wheels with forged alloy rims were supplied by OZ.

A major goal of the Anniversary exercise was to make the Countach a more habitable supercar. Gone were the previous seats, which looked as if they had been swiped from the *Star Wars* set; in their place were less dramatic looking buckets that were more comfortable and featured a power-seat-back recline. The steering wheel also was replaced. A new, more powerful air conditioner that could hold its own against the greenhouse effect of the steeply raked windshield finally was fitted, and the front-door half windows got electric lifts, at last.

While the changes did shave off some of the car's rough edges—and hinted at the character of its succes-

Though the ungainly front bumper was retained on U.S. models, the rear fascia was redesigned to incorporate a real bumper (*top right*). The car also got revised sail-panel scoops and vents and new rocker panel strakes (*right*).

sor—they did not alter the Countach's basic bare-knuckles approach. This was confirmed by Gordon Murray, who evaluated a 25th Anniversary Countach in *Motor Trend* in July 1990. "Simply sitting in the Lambo, there's a supercar feel, a sense of occasion missing from the Porsche," Murray said. "The way the [gullwing] doors open, and particularly the way they close, is wonderful: They scythe down and shut you in with a solid 'clomp.'

"When I first tried to drive away, I had to open the door and ask if the throttle had a lock on it!" he said. "The throttle's about the same weight as a 911's clutch, and the clutch is even heavier than a 911's, which is saying something. The combination of these things and the stiffness and balking of the gear change actually prevent you from driving the Countach properly. On the track, I was always worried about getting the gear before the next corner.... Okay, it [the V-12 engine] doesn't have that electrifying surge that startles you the first time you reach the [twin-turbo] Porsche's powerband, but it revs freely and has a much more punchy feel right through the range. And I think that's important."

Factory acceleration figures for the 25th Anniversary Edition (0-60 mph in 4.7 seconds and a 12.9-second quarter-mile) eclipse those obtained by outside testers of previous Countachs. The fac-

In front the 25th Anniversary Countach got a new spoiler and color coordinated side-view mirrors (*top*). Engine output was the same as the previous year's 5000 QV, but the new vents (*bottom*) increased cooling capacity and overheating tendencies were reduced.

tory's top speed of 183.3 mph (in 5th gear at 7300 rpm) was only a tad slower than the 185 mph Bob Wallace said he saw in an early model.

So the Anniversary Edition not only was the most comfortable Countach ever, it very likely was the fastest production example. And with 650 built by the end of production in July 1990, it also turned out to be the biggest seller. In fact, Lamborghini had planned to produce only about 300 25th Anniversary Countachs, but sales took off. Several factors contributed to this, including a red-hot supercar market, collector interest, quality and driveability improvements wrought with Chrysler's

help, and delays in the Countach's successor. Continued improvement is what kept the Countach viable in increasingly hostile times. That's another reason demand for it never abated, even though 15 years of inflation and mechanical alterations more than tripled its original U.S. price of around $45,000.

The Countach will always be an utter contradiction: an awesome, stunning, entirely useless, absolutely incredible racer-for-the road. it was a futuristic machine built the old-fashioned way. It will be a long, long time before a car has a greater impact on the world.

model	1974-78 Countach LP 400	1978-82 Countach LP 400 S	1982-85 Countach LP 5000 S	1985-88 Countach LP 5000 QV	1988-90 25th Anniv. Ed.
production	150	235	323	610	650
engine	dohc V-12	dohc V-12	dohc V-12	dohc V-12	dohc V-12
displacement cc/ci	3929/240	3929/240	4754/290	5167/315	5167/315
horsepower @ RPM (DIN)	375 @ 8000	375 @ 8000	375 @ 7000	420[1] @ 7000	455 @ 7000
torque @ RPM (lbs/ft)	286 @ 5000	285 @ 5000	302 @ 4500	340[1] @ 5000	369 @ 5200
length (mm/in.)	4140/161.5	4140/161.5	4140/161.5	4240/165.4	4240/165.4
width (mm/in.)	1890/73.7	2000/78	2000/78	2000/78	2017/78.6
height (mm/in.)	1070/41.7	1070/41.7	1070/41.7	1070/41.7	1070/41.7
wheelbase (mm/in.)	2450/95.5	2450/95.5	2450/95.5	2473/96.5	2473/96.5
track, front (mm/in.)	1500/58.5	1490/58.1	1492/58.2	1535/59.9	1535/59.9
track, rear (mm/in.)	1520/59.3	1605/62.5	1606/62.6	1606/62.6	1606/62.6
weight (kg/lbs)[2]	1300/2860	1360/2992	1480/3256	1568/3450	1568/3450

[1]Numbers were later revised to 455 bhp @ 7000 and 369 lbs/ft @ 5200.
[2]Factory dry-weight claims, actual numbers higher.

CHAPTER SEVEN

URRACO

LAMBORGHINI'S ONLY ATTEMPT

AT MASS-MARKET PRODUCTION

WAS A DISMAL FAILURE BY MOST

STANDARDS. HOWEVER, THE CAR

IT PRODUCED, THE URRACO,

WAS VASTLY UNDERRATED.

Throughout its history, Lamborghini had established itself with big, world-class GTs for the very wealthy. However, the economic climate was changing quickly in the late 1960s, and one of the best-selling sports cars in Italy was the Porsche 911. Then, in 1967 Ferrari unveiled its new 206 Dino, and suddenly Lamborghini was behind the times. These two cars were smaller and more efficient than the big road-hugging V-12s coming out of Maranello and Sant'Agata. Ferruccio Lamborghini was not one to pass up an opportunity, so, in typical fashion, he quickly moved toward volume production of a car he hoped would surpass the other two in almost every way.

The firm had shown interest early on in a smaller, less costly, and more widely saleable car. Guests at *Il Cavaliere's* first major open house, at the time of the 1963 Turin show, were told of plans for either a V-8 or perhaps an inline slant-six derived from his 3.5-liter V-12, suggesting that a "junior" model would be offered one day.

The main reason Ferruccio wanted a "budget" Lamborghini was survival. A more affordable, higher-volume offering would be the great leap forward by which a small, vulnerable "boutique" automaker could become a larger, more broadly-based concern better able to weather economic storms. The prime example was Porsche. The once-tiny German sports-car maker had become a growing force in the European military/industrial complex by 1967. Sant'Agata's managers apparently envisioned Lamborghini following suit,

perhaps establishing a similar engineering consultation business and supplying components to other automakers, and certainly fielding a wider product range of its own.

Since the mid-engine Miura was making money and the big four-seat Espada had been launched, it seemed the time had come to pursue the expansionist dream. Paolo Stanzani took over as head of both engineering and plant management in 1968, and it was soon afterward—certainly during 1969—that he and his staff began drawing up the new volume model. What emerged—a compact 2+2 with a new small-capacity V-8 mounted amidships—would be Lamborghini's first direct entry into the lucrative market inhabited by cars like the Porsche 911 and Ferrari's Dino 246 GT.

For Stanzani, this was the first chance to create an all-new car of his own, and he made the most of it. Jean-Francois Marchet has described him as "a wise and clear-sighted man" who "likes very clean designs and direct solutions, even if this sometimes makes them more complicated to achieve." Lamborghini's new baby thus arrived with a distinct design elegance inside and out, especially in its engine and chassis.

Rather than starting with the Bizzarrini-designed V-12, Stanzani had a completely new engine drawn up. His aim was a powerplant that would be easier and less costly to build, tractable in traffic, easier to maintain in extended service, and adaptable for the pollution controls then being man-

dated. What emerged was a 90-degree V-8 with a displacement of 2462.9 cubic centimeters on an 86-millimeter bore and a 53-mm stroke.

This "L240" unit was a graceful piece of work, and very light (375 pounds) thanks to an aluminum block and heads. It wasn't especially exotic, though. Rubber belts drove a single overhead camshaft per head, and the two valves for each cylinder were parallel and in line with the cylinder axis. Combustion chambers were formed via concave piston crowns. This type of arrangement, called Heron head, offers certain benefits for both manufacturing and emissions control Compression ratio was set at 10.5:1.

On the dyno, the L240 thrummed out 220 DIN horsepower at 7500 rpm and 166 pounds/feet torque at 5750—impressive numbers that amounted to the same 89 bhp/liter produced by the V-12.

The neat little L240 power package was designed to mount sideways ahead of the rear wheels, much like the Miura installation except that the V-8's shorter crankshaft allowed the five-speed transmission to extend beyond the engine on the left, in line with the crank. This, in turn, allowed a direct run for shift linkage to the selector mechanism, a distinct improvement on the Miura's.

That selector mechanism was on the bottom of the transmission because the two gearshafts were on the same level, the output shaft to the rear. As the output shaft in turn engaged the final-drive gearwheel (which extended to

Making its debut at the 1970 Turin motor show, the Urraco (*above*) looked like an exotic car, but was very practical. The engine (*far left*) was an entirely new design created by Paolo Stanzani. It was a 2462 cc V-8 with only one camshaft per bank of cylinders and put out 220 bhp at 7500 rpm. Locating the powerplant in the rear allowed the front boot (*left*) to carry the spare tire and a few extra bags.

the rear), there were only three basic rotation centers—crank, second transmission shaft, and final drive. The crankshaft thus rotated "forward" in the same direction as the rear wheels.

Designated P 250 (P again denoting *posterior*), the new chassis was a sheet-steel unibody structure like the Espada's. Within a wheelbase of 2450 mm (96.5 inches), Stanzani found room for two people in front and two short-term guests in back. He managed this although at 26 inches, the sidewinder V-8 was five inches "longer" across the heads than the Miura's V-12. Front-seaters had to angle their legs a bit because of wheel-arch intrusion, and seating the rear was cramped. However, the packaging was quite efficient.

Suspension design was part of the trick. Like many other automakers, Lamborghini realized that the compact MacPherson strut freed up much volume, and decided to install one at each corner. (In Japan, Nissan had just

done the same for its nifty little Datsun 240Z.) However, all-round struts are less than ideal for a high-performance car, as they force the wheels to lean with body roll, and suffer friction and rigidity problems. Lamborghini was determined to make the geometry work, and Bob Wallace did. In a cost-saving move with an eye toward mass production, several key parts were produced by outside suppliers. The MacPherson struts were borrowed from Fiat's top-of-the-line 130, and brakes came from BMW.

Body design was still an out-of-house matter. As Lamborghini wanted something special for its new car, it commissioned Bertone to make up not one but two separate prototypes. The designs were adequate, but not what Ferruccio was looking for, so a third attempt was made. That proved to be the charm, and the production P 250 emerged as a genuine beauty—that rare blend of balance, delicacy, grace,

innovation, and passion that never seems to age. As a finishing touch, someone came up with another bull-fighting name: Urraco—appropriately, "young bull." So christened, the car was first unveiled at the Turin show in late 1970.

Response was highly favorable and orders started coming in right away. Unfortunately, this all-new design needed heavy refinement before it would be production-ready. This development time took nearly two years, and during this time customers began canceling.

This was unfortunate, because everything was starting to fall apart for *Automobili Ferruccio Lamborghini*. The man whose name graced the factory was losing his interest as fast as his money, and the work force was increasingly restive. In addition, the Urraco program faced its own difficulties. Because it had been predicated on higher sales than previous Lambor-

Lamborghini produced three versions of the Urraco from 1972-79. The P 300 (*below*) was fitted with a new engine with greater displacement and two more camshafts. This revised engine added 30 bhp and pounds/feet of torque. This model sold in decent numbers, and the motoring press gave glowing reviews, but the car failed to find a niche and was discontinued in 1979.

ghinis, the firm had invested heavily in new machine tools and factory space for it. The sales forecasts quickly proved optimistic, which meant that unit cost would increase.

In the end, it was the many and major teething problems that hurt the P 250 most. Beside engine and suspension failures, there were difficulties with cam-drive belts, transmission, cooling system, and tires. As if all that

weren't enough, it was decided at the 11th hour to redo the interior to facilitate assembly of the right-hand-drive version.

When production finally got underway, it did so at a snail's pace: 35 units through the end of 1972 and 285 for all of '73—a far cry from the hoped-for 1000 a year. As for the few buyers who took delivery, they discovered that not all the gremlins had been exorcized from their long-awaited Urracos.

In 1974, Ferruccio severed all ties with his company, and Swiss owners Rossetti and Leimer put Stanzani in charge of day-to-day operations. They gave the go-ahead to implement fundamental revisions. Because sales volume was down, price would have to go up. This dictated that quality and

"Urraco Bob" rides to the rescue

There was a Urraco fully worthy of the marque—one so unique that Sant'Agata workers gave it a special name: "Urraco Bob." As the name suggests, it was the third of Bob Wallace's personal hot rods.

This "super-sports" Urraco was never an official factory project. It was, however, the most elaborate and far-reaching of the three.

With a leftover pre-production prototype as its starting point, the Rally Urraco piece-by-piece became a very thoroughly honed competition instrument. Wallace stripped it of all unnecessary weight, then added a judicious bit back by welding stiffeners and a roll cage into the structure. Steel was replaced with aluminum wherever possible. To sharpen handling, he solidly bolted in the powertrain/rear suspension subframe. A large fuel tank went in where the rear seats had been, and wider wheels and tires were added. Offering 310 bhp in final form, it was very fast.

"Over the years it ended up with a variety of odds and ends," Wallace recalls now, "including a six-speed transaxle and a dry-sump, four-valve, three-liter engine, and we even put a wing on it. It was an extremely quick and extremely good-handling car. In fact, the one and only time we ever raced it, at Misano, down by the Adriatic coast, I lapped everyone."

performance would have to increase proportionately.

To compound the problems, a new "mini-midi" Ferrari, the 308 GT4, had arrived in 1973 with a transverse 3.0-liter V-8 and a Bertone body. Responding to this direct competition, Sant'Agata enlarged the Urraco V-8 to the same level—actually 2997 cc/182.8 cubic inches—via a longer 64.5-mm (2.54-inch) stroke, and completely revised its top end via new heads. Reliable chains drove four camshafts, and combustion chambers were now in the heads. On slightly reduced 10.0:1 compression, this L300 unit pumped out a claimed 250 bhp DIN at 7500 rpm and 195 pounds/feet of torque at 3500.

This new car, the P 300, made its debut at the 1974 Turin show. It was a much-improved Urraco in many ways, with numerous detail changes to transmission, suspension, and bodywork.

The factory pronounced it good for more than 160 mph flat out, and those with experience believed it. Automotive journalist Pete Lyons took a brief drive in an example and found it a delightfully sparkling little car. Thanks to years of hard flogging by the sensitive and determined Bob Wallace, many European connoisseurs judged the P 300 one of the best-handling cars around. The Urraco's promise seemed fulfilled.

The car was still off-target and Lamborghini's declining fortunes precluded the modifications necessary to legalize the P 300 for the American market. Instead, U.S. Urracos continued with the sohc 2.5, detoxed to an anemic 180 bhp.

Beginning in 1975, there was also a P 200 Urraco, a home-market special created in response to new Italian tax laws that levied very heavy penalties

In addition to its larger engine, the Urraco P 300 (*above*) received a vastly revised suspension. Many journalists listed it as the best handling car in Europe. Due to the tight packaging, Lamborghini was forced to go with a V-8 engine (*below*) in the Urraco. The transmission was bolted directly to the end of the engine and the V-8 profile created a very compact package.

on cars with engines above 2.0 liters. This carried the original sohc L250 engine debored to 77.4 mm for a displacement of 1995 cc. Claimed power was 182 DIN at 7500 rpm.

Although 791 Urracos were built between 1972 and 1979, the car never lived up to its potential. The rush to production, fuel crises, and development problems all led to its downfall. However, the clean sheet approach taken by Stanzani would bear fruit for the future.

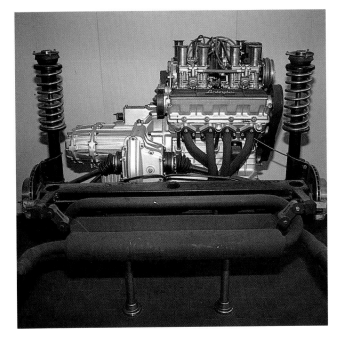

model	1972-76 Urraco P 250	1975-77 Urraco P 200	1975-79 Urraco P 300
production	520	66	205
engine	sohc V-8	sohc V-8	dohc V-8
displacement cc/ci	2462/150	1994/122	2996/183
horsepower @ RPM (DIN)	220 @ 7500	182 @ 7500	250 @ 7500
torque @ RPM (lbs/ft)	166 @ 5750	130 @ 3800	195 @ 5750
length (mm/in.)	4250/165.8	4250/165.8	4250/165.8
width (mm/in.)	1760/68.6	1760/68.6	1760/68.6
height (mm/in.)	1160/45.2	1160/42.5	1160/45.2
wheelbase (mm/in.)	2450/95.5	2450/95.5	2450/95.5
track, front (mm/in.)	1460/57	1450/57	1450/56.5
track, rear (mm/in.)	1460/57	1450/57	1470/57.3
weight (kg/lbs)[1]	1100/2420	1250/2750	1280/2816

[1]Factory dry-weight claims, actual numbers higher.

CHAPTER EIGHT

SILHOUETTE, JALPA, LM002

THE '70s WERE A TIME OF SEVERE

ECONOMIC TROUBLES AT

LAMBORGHINI, BUT OUT OF IT

CAME THREE FINE VEHICLES. THE

SILHOUETTE AND JALPA UPDATED

THE URRACO CHASSIS, WHILE THE

HUGE LM002 LITERALLY BROKE

NEW GROUND FOR LAMBORGHINI.

Lamborghini was not the only specialty automaker to experience economic troubles in the '70s, Ferrari had piles of unsold Dinos and de Tomaso had to temporarily shut down production, but the problems at *Automobili Ferruccio Lamborghini SpA* had gotten so bad by 1978 that a loan was granted by the Italian government just to keep production of existing cars moving. It is a wonder any new models were developed during this era. Yet as a strange twist of fate, the development of these new projects was one of the main causes for the company's cash crunch.

After Rossetti and Leimer obtained full control of the Lamborghini from Ferruccio in 1974, they needed a person to take over day-to-day operations. When it became apparent that engineer Paolo Stanzani needed help, they called upon Pier Luigi Capellini. Capellini came over from de Tomaso at a time when that company was floundering, and his first order of business was to sell a stockpile of remaining Urracos. He did this in short order by pushing the P 200, and then hired a new chief engineer, Franco Baraldini. These two men then set out to try to raise money for Lamborghini.

Baraldini made two attempts to obtain contract work. One was unsuccessful and the other only partly successful. First, he obtained a contract to build the chassis and running gear for BMW's fantastic new M1. At the same time, an effort was made to land the U.S. military bid to build a replacement for the venerable Jeep—a project Lamborghini would call the Cheetah.

While all of this activity was going on, there was continued demand for the Countach and spasmodic production of Espadas, Jaramas, Silhouettes, and Urracos, but these cars were barely paying for themselves. New cash would have to be found to finance the M1 and Jeep projects. Capellini tried to get Rossetti and Leimer to sell out to Canadian oil magnate Walter Wolf, but they could not agree on price. Frustrated, Capellini asked for, and received, a loan from the Italian government for £1 million. However, this was not enough to support both projects.

Leimer and Baraldini decided to invest the money in the Cheetah project, and when BMW found out they quickly pulled the plug on Lamborghini. Then the Cheetah project panned. Later, Capellini would go on to set up a separate company to handle the BMW project, but the money was gone. Lamborghini went into receivership.

Amidst all of this came the introduction of a new Lamborghini model. In 1976 Lamborghini introduced the Silhouette at the Geneva auto show. Though it was based on the Urraco platform, the car carried an entirely new design.

The big change to the car was a roof reworked into a "targa" style. The panel above the seats was removable and could be stored behind the seats.

The Urraco's fastback became a notched "tunnelback" design and rear side windows were deleted. Stylish side scoops finished in a contrasting color were added to provide visual relief for the resulting massive rear quarters. Squared-up flared wheel arches shrouded Pirelli's state-of-the-art P7 tires on wider-than-Urraco wheels with the five-hole "telephone dial" design first seen on Bertone's Urraco-based 1974 Bravo one-off. Further disguising the Urraco lower body was a more angular nose and a deeper front spoiler that incorporated an oil-cooler duct and front-brake air scoops. Inside was a new, more ergonomic dash.

Underneath was a P 300 unit body/chassis structure suitably strengthened to go topless, including a safety roll cage within the rear roof area. The P 300 powertrain was carried over unaltered. Weight dropped by 88 pounds, so performance and road manners promised to be at least the equal of the P 300's, if not better.

Many people found the Silhouette's looks to their liking, and the car enjoyed a favorable reception. "From most angles, it's a very pretty car," wrote Sue Ransom of Australia's *Modern Motor*, "and, in my view, more attractive than the Urraco."

Several made it across through the gray market, and *Car and Driver*'s Pat Bedard tried one modified to appease the EPA and found a lot for a car enthu-

siast to like. The suspension pleased him: smooth, supple, and bereft of harshness despite the wide super-performance tires. "Somebody at Lamborghini knows about suspension."

As for the engine, he said, "The catalytic converter smothers the exhaust note, choking it right down to civilized volumes, but the sound is still pure high-calorie Italian: whirring cam drives, sucking carburetors, rattling transmission bearings.... The eight carburetor barrels sing like organ pipes, and the patter of all those valves opening and closing blends together into a sweet, mechanical moan.... It's *Sounds of Sebring* all over again, live and in color. We are red and we are on the move."

With all this plus open-air appeal, the Silhouette should have sold well. It didn't, and the reasons weren't hard to pinpoint.

Though dumping the Urraco's back seat made for a "purer" sports car, the designers were unable to reconfigure the cockpit for the sort of space around the pedals that Miura drivers enjoyed. There was no money for that. So the two-seater had to retain the Urraco's floorpan and basic bodyshell, including windshield and surrounding structure. That meant it inherited not only

most of the Urraco's design faults, but the same indifferent workmanship and suspect reliability.

The telling blow was the fact that Lamborghini was in no position to certify the Silhouette for the American market. Inevitably, then, demand never approached hoped-for levels, and the creaky Sant'Agata line ground out a grand total of 52 Silhouettes before sputtering to a halt as corporate arteries hardened in the late '70s.

Despite the turmoil at Lamborghini in the late-'70s, the company managed to field a new product—the Silhouette—in 1976. Based on the worthy Urraco chassis, the Silhouette featured Lamborghini's first-ever open roof design (*top*). Wheel arches were added to accommodate larger tires and the Urraco's rear louvers were dropped in favor of a Countach-like tunnel-back engine cover (*above*). However, only 52 Silhouettes were built and the car was never officially certified for American sale.

It was 1978 and *Automobili Ferruccio Lamborghini SpA* fell under the control of the Italian authorities, a last desperate step before bankruptcy. After many rumors, a buyer was finally found. The Mimram brothers, who had made their fortunes in commerce and shipping, appointed Patrick Mimram as president. Mimram was a young, 'blue jeans' type who brought hope to the new Lamborghini.

The first evidence of this was the release of a new little Lambo. Engineer Giulio Alfieri came over from Maserati and picked up where Stanzani had left off a few years earlier. He lengthened the V-8's stroke to 75 millimeters (2.95 inches) for a new displacement of 3485 cubic centimeters (213 cubic inches). That bumped power to 255 DIN at 7000 rpm and peak torque to 231 pounds/feet at 3500.

Several Silhouettes made it to America through the gray market (*top*). The powertrain was mostly a carryover from the Urraco P 300. However, weight was down by almost 100 pounds and the tires were larger so performance was up. The car's five-hole wheels, were first seen on the Bertone show car, Bravo. The removable targa-roof panel could be stored behind the front seats.

Inside, the rear seats were removed in favor of a parcel shelf; a roll cage was added to account for the loss of the roof; and dash and interior were substantially reworked. The new interior was finally worthy of a Lamborghini and gauges and controls that had been spread across the Urraco dash were now grouped in front of the driver. Bumpers were neatly incorporated into the front and rear design—a marked change from the Countach of this era.

In addition, some internal transmission ratios were juggled to suit, suspension details revamped, and even lower-profile P7s were specified on larger, 16-inch-diameter wheels (versus the previous 15s). Cosmetic alterations were made to the fender flares, nose, C-pillars, and there was another new interior treatment. There was also a new name: Jalpa, another breed of toro. The new-breed Lamborghini went on sale in 1982.

It was well received. "As a model for rebuilding Lamborghini's reputation, it stands a good chance," was J-F Marchet's optimistic assessment. Although the steering was heavy at low speeds, he continued, "The Jalpa was very easy to drive in varied conditions, and...it was suitable for city traffic."

Road & Track judged the Jalpa "one of the most exciting cars to drive we've come across in recent years...an exotic car that demands a firm and knowledgeable hand at the wheel—then it delivers more driving excitement than many of us experience in a lifetime." Said excitement translated to 7.3 seconds for the 0-60 charge, and to 15.4 seconds at 92 mph in the standing quarter-mile. On the down side, the cabin was still quite uncomfortable, fuel consumption was an estimated 12 mpg, and the price had crept up to a cool $58,000.

It's true the price was quite high, but the car offered a solid sense of everyday value. "In essence," wrote auto writer Pete Lyons, "this is a Practical Exotic—a super-expensive automotive toy that is willing to work for its living. As sensuous to look at as an Italian starlet, its bodywork is of sturdy steel. Low-slung as a stalking cat, it's com-

fortable and content in civilized traffic streams. Its motor, mounted midships like a racer, is a wondrous, raucous thing of many camshafts housed in light alloys; yet its personality is docile, broad-shouldered and friendly."

Jalpa sales, never strong to begin with, tailed off through 1989. Eventually 410 were produced, making the car a moderate success. However, the Jalpa was always the "other" car built by Lamborghini, for few cars if any were able to eclipse the mighty Countach. There was, however, one vehicle that was just as outrageous—the LM-Series.

The LM originated in 1977 during the period when Lamborghini was desperately seeking enough work and money to stay alive. Franco Baraldini secured a contract with the American firm Mobility Technology International to design and produce an all-terrain runabout for sale to the U.S. military under its High Utility Mobile Military Vehicle (HUMMV) program. This program was set up to devise a replacement for the World War II-vintage Jeep.

The resulting prototype was called the Cheetah, an odd-looking, Jeep-like truck with a rear-mounted, 360-cubic-inch Chrysler V-8 and automatic transmission. However, Mobility Technol-

After the Silhouette's dismal production run of only 52 units, the Jalpa arrived in 1982 to put some spark back into the junior Lamborghini. While appearing not much different on the outside, the Jalpa was a new car underneath the skin. Suspension, transmission, engine, and interior changes highlighted the new model. Outside, fender flares were rounded, the rear flanks were softened, and new wheels were added. Inside, a new even-better dash replaced the fairly comprehensive Silhouette version.

ogy ran into patent infringement trouble with FMC Corporation, maker of the eventual HUMMV, and had to abandon the project. This left Lamborghini with a $25,000-per-unit military vehicle that was not all that good and even less saleable. Complicating matters even further, the prototype was destroyed in a crash during a demonstration in the California desert.

This left Lamborghini in a dire financial situation. Rossetti and Leimer had diverted the loan from the Italian government away from the M1 program and to the now-dead Cheetah project. BMW quickly scrambled to find other contractors. As you will remember, Capellini set up a company to get the M1 into production, and the Italian government put Lamborghini into receivership. Then the Mimram brothers showed up and pumped a healthy dose of cash into the program.

The idea of a super off-roader made a good deal of sense to the new owners. They were from Switzerland and an upscale off-road-type vehicle might just do well in their native land. Thus stoked, the fire flared up at the 1981 Geneva show with an all-new, all-Lamborghini, all-terrain vehicle.

Well, almost all-Lamborghini. This second iteration, called LM001 (the letters are explained as meaning either "Lamborghini Military" or "Lamborghini-Mimram"), was supposed to be available with either a 4.75-liter Countach V-12 or 360-cid AMC V-8. Either way, it was still a rear-engine design that had some marked deficiencies. The main problem seemed to be that weight transfer in acceleration made the front end too light for steering control. Lamborghini came up with a solution in a third vehicle with the engine in front.

The result, called LMA (A for *Anteriore*, referring to the front engine), appeared in 1982. Beside significant revisions to suspension and chassis, it also had power steering and could carry extra people where the engine had been in the Cheetah and 001. All this worked much better in testing and the LMA began looking like a promising commercial prospect—so much so that it was redesignated LM002 in anticipation of series production.

The LM002 had a wheelbase of over three meters (118.1 inches). Track measured 63.6 inches front and rear. Overall length was 191.1 inches, width 78.7, and height a rangy 69.8 inches. Ground clearance was 11.6 inches. A steel-tube space frame supported an all-independent coil-spring suspension. Rolling stock consisted of 17-inch steel wheels mounting 325/65VR tires. Brakes were discs at the front, drums in back. The engine was a version of the Countach *Quattrovalvole*. At 5167 cc, with Weber carbs, and 9.5:1 compression, it packed 444 bhp at 6800 rpm and 368 pounds/feet of torque at 4500 rpm.

Because this was a Lamborghini, the LM's four-door notchback body was made of lightweight aluminum and fiberglass. Belying the square-rigged utilitarian styling was an interior upholstered in fine leather and furnished as to give the uncanny impression of a giant, upright Countach. Fuel capacity was a camel-like 76.6 gallons.

An extremely heavy-duty ZF five-speed gearbox and two-speed transfer case made up the four-wheel-drive system. The front hubs had to be

locked manually for 4WD operation, which seemed a bit old-fashioned. On the other hand, the transfer box had a very cunning design that allowed the front wheels to turn one percent faster than the rears, which enhanced stability and traction in the dirt.

Though the original idea was to sell the LM to various armies, Lamborghini began to develop a decent civilian mar-ket for the LM—wealthy clients who'd really rather drive a Countach but who lived in places with few paved roads. That meant sheikhs and the like—even a few Americans.

Car and Driver's Brock Yates experi-enced the range of LM capabilities in an American-spec model during the summer of 1987. "Rambo Lambo," he called it. "Meet the closest thing to a street-legal Tiger tank known to man," he wrote. "Never before in recent memory have we driven a vehicle that has turned as many heads, blown as many minds, freaked as many citizens, or been as much insane, outrageous fun."

Yates went on to point out the LM tested had, "the standard Italian exotic's complement of wacky contra-

For the first time a Lamborghini was constructed, from the outset, with American safety concerns in mind. The Jalpa had integrated front and rear bumpers and a revised rear fascia (*top*) to accommodate U.S. regulations. The new engine, at 3485 cc, was larger than the Silhouette motor, and slightly more powerful. At 255 bhp, the Jalpa engine (*bottom left*) was actually much more powerful because it made that horsepower while satisfying U.S. emissions regulations— something the Silhouette never had to do. Torque was up substantially to 235 pounds/feet. The new engine, coupled with a revised suspension, made the Jalpa the first Lamborghini that was easy to drive in urban conditions.

Nineteen eighty-eight was the last year for the Jalpa—and for all smaller Lamborghinis for that matter (*right*). Rumors persisted at Sant'Agata that a V-10 replacement was in the works, but no such model ever appeared. Way back in 1977, Lamborghini put together a Jeep replacement for the U.S. Army using a rear-mounted, 360-cubic-inch Chrysler V-8 as a powerplant. The result was called the Cheetah (*below*). This vehicle was never produced and was destroyed in testing.

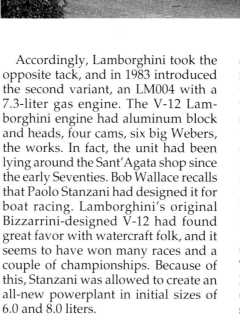

dictions and absurdities," everything from non-cancelling turn signals to air conditioning that pumped hot air. He also complained that steering and clutch effort was heavy at low speed.

But on the prowl, "Rambo" was a savage joy: "Once the tach needle sweeps past 5000 rpm, the LM002 sheds its street clothes and begins to operate like something out of DC Comics. The big engine howls unearthly tones through its dual exhausts, and suddenly one is seeking out 3-series BMWs, Mustangs, and Z28 Camaros. To shock and humiliate their hapless drivers is one of the more civilized urges one gets behind the wheel of this leviathan."

This biggest Lamborghini handled and braked remarkably well. Off road, "the surprisingly supple Lambo suspension soaked up the impacts like a sprinting tiger. The brute is pure feline when it comes to rapid off-road transit—truly the best such machine we have ever encountered."

Against *C&D*'s computerized test gear, Yates' 002 did 0-60 mph in 7.7 seconds, the standing quarter-mile in 16.0 seconds at 86 mph, and 118 mph all-out. The full-throttle sound reading was 97 dBA, not quite as loud as the vintage Miura. However, observed mpg was a lowly 8.

Production of the LM002 ceased in 1993. From the vehicle's introduction in 1982 until the last 4×4 rolled out, the factory production totaled 301. The final 60 were tagged the LM/American. They share the LM002 mechanical specifications, but were dressed out in commemorative badging and body stripes, as rolled on MSW/OZ Racing alloy wheels.

There were two variants of the LM002 Series, both engine conversions. The first was a version developed with a 3.0-liter turbocharged diesel six supplied by Italy's VM. Since this engine offered only 150 bhp to carry nearly three tons, this LM003 literally went nowhere.

Accordingly, Lamborghini took the opposite tack, and in 1983 introduced the second variant, an LM004 with a 7.3-liter gas engine. The V-12 Lamborghini engine had aluminum block and heads, four cams, six big Webers, the works. In fact, the unit had been lying around the Sant'Agata shop since the early Seventies. Bob Wallace recalls that Paolo Stanzani had designed it for boat racing. Lamborghini's original Bizzarrini-designed V-12 had found great favor with watercraft folk, and it seems to have won many races and a couple of championships. Because of this, Stanzani was allowed to create an all-new powerplant in initial sizes of 6.0 and 8.0 liters.

As used in the LM004, this powerhouse displaced precisely 7257 cubic centimeters (443 cubic inches). Claimed power output was 420 DIN at 5400 rpm, torque was 435 pounds/feet at 3500 rpm.

Britain's *Autocar* tested the LM004 in May 1986. Needless to say, the staff was quite impressed. Driving through a water basin [20-inches deep] proved no problem, no water entered through the doors, although they were under water." With typical British understatement, *Autocar* noted that the LM's "ability to take steep hills is unprecedented....It can take a single angle of 70 degrees without falling over, although that isn't very comfortable for passengers. One has to depend very much on the car, since the only thing you can see is the [hood]."

As for performance, the LM004 was tested properly only by the factory. They claimed top speed of over 200 km/h (125 mph) and 0-100 km/h (0-62-mph) time of "no more than 8.5 seconds." These were highly impressive numbers. Despite all the clamor, Lamborghini built only one LM004.

Though the market for the LM series remained small, this outrageous vehicle's impact has always been large. It provided some needed cash into the coffers at a time when there was none. Sometimes good things come in *big* packages.

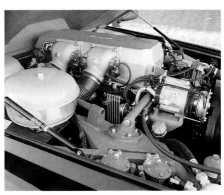

The Cheetah project did not die, however; in 1982 Lamborghini unleashed the LM002 (*above*). This was an all-new design with Countach V-12 placed in front. This monster motor made 455 bhp and 360 pounds/feet of torque. Offering four-wheel drive and imposing looks, the LM002 became somewhat of a legend in its own right. The truck could reach 60 mph from a standstill in 7.7 seconds and topped out at 118 mph. The rear cargo bay (*bottom right*) could accommodate four extra passengers or miscellaneous equipment. Sales of the LM002 were surprisingly good and 301 were built over the vehicle's 12-year life span.

model	1976-78 Silhouette	1982-88 Jalpa	1982-93 LM002
production	52	410	301
engine	dohc V-8	dohc V-8	dohc V-12
displacement cc/ci	2996/183	3485/213	5167/315
horsepower @ RPM (DIN)	250 @ 7500	255 @ 7000	444 @ 6800
torque @ RPM (lbs/ft)	195 @ 5750	235 @ 3250	368 @ 6800
length (mm/in.)	4320/168.5	4330/168.9	4900/191.1
width (mm/in.)	1880/73.3	1880/73.3	2000/78.7
height (mm/in.)	1120/43.7	1140/44.5	1790/69.8
wheelbase (mm/in.)	2450/95.5	2450/99.6	3028/118.1
track, front (mm/in.)	1490/58	1500/58.5	1615/63.6
track, rear (mm/in.)	1550/60.5	1554/60.6	1616/63.6
weight (kg/lbs)[1]	1240/2728	1502/3305	3034/6675

[1]Factory dry-weight claims, actual numbers higher.

CHAPTER NINE

DIABLO

AFTER ALMOST 16 YEARS OF

PRODUCTION, THE MIGHTY

COUNTACH FINALLY GAVE WAY

TO A SUCCESSOR. IT WAS A

CAR WORTHY OF THE COUNTACH

HERITAGE IN EVERY WAY.

IT WAS HEAVEN AND HELL ON

EARTH. IT WAS DIABLO.

The task of replacing the Countach must have seemed nearly impossible to Lamborghini designers and engineers. Styling on the Countach was barbaric, performance was awe-inspiring, and sales were tremendous. In addition, the Lamborghini team faced a changing automotive world. Fuel economy had suddenly become important. Also, governments were enacting tough emissions and safety regulations that made it extremely difficult for a small car maker to turn a profit. Despite all of this, Lamborghini developed their most devious model yet, the Diablo.

In 1985 stylists began working on a design replacement for the Countach. The earlier Miura and the Countach had broken the sports car mold with sensuous styling, inspired engineering, and a barbaric lust for speed. They were products of designers who had allowed their imaginations to flow. In a sense, those gathered at Sant'Agata back in '85 needed only to duplicate that feeling—certainly no easy task.

To simply unleash their creativity would be of little use to the Lamborghini team. The world had changed. No longer was it enough that each supercar be merely faster and more outrageous than the last. Emissions concerns and safety issues were now part of the blueprint, as were reliability, assembly quality, even a certain degree of refinement. To these demands Lamborghini management added yet another requirement: Not

only must the Countach's successor meet the regulatory standards of every market in which it sold, its performance had to be the same world-over. About the only thing that *hadn't* changed was that the new Lamborghini would have to be worthy of carrying the torch passed from the Miura to the Countach. This new car had to be an automobile so savage in sound and manner, so idiosyncratic, so alive that it could evoke thoughts of both heaven and hell.

Behold the Diablo: A name not only meaning 'devil,' but also an illustrious breed of Spanish fighting bull. Lamborghini knew better than to wander from its roots in nomenclature, and it stuck to a proven formula in engineering as well. The Diablo, like the Countach, has a longitudinally mounted midships V-12 with the gearbox located ahead of the engine. However, the new car is larger and heavier than the Countach. It has a bigger engine, additional amenities, and more sophisticated componentry.

"It was no easy task to replace the world's most famous supercar," said Lamborghini President Emile Novaro. "When we began the program back in June 1985, my instructions to the team were to make it better than the Countach. Better performance, safety, comfort, visibility, accessibility, and emissions. And give me at least 315 km/h (196.5 mph)."

When introduced, Lamborghini claimed the Diablo's top speed to be

202 mph, 19 mph above that of the 25th Anniversary Countach. Independent testing backed this claim, and the Diablo became the fastest production car in the world. Its top end betters the Ferrari F40, for which its maker claims a 201-mph top speed, and the Porsche 959, with its manufacturer's rating of 197 mph. Ferrari's Testarossa, the only other exotic with a mid-engine V-12, tops out at 178. Since the Diablo's introduction, Bugatti and several other makers have touted cars that supposedly top out higher than the Diablo. However, the Bugatti EB110 is the only model with a tested speed above 202 mph, and, believe it or not, its price is almost twice as high.

With the Diablo, Lamborghini closed a debate about the style and substance of the Countach's successor that had simmered at Sant'Agata since the Patrick Mimran days of the early 1980s. That's when Lamborghini brought in Luigi Marmiroli as technical director. His credentials included building his own independent design company and stints in the upper management of Ferrari and Alfa Romeo.

For the basic design of the new car, Marmiroli turned to Marcello Gandini, the man who had fashioned both the Miura and the Countach. Gandini started work in November of '85 and by May '86 had set down what he envisioned as the car's final shape. The creation retained its predecessor's spirit, but where the Countach celebrated the wedge, Gandini's new machine

showed a decidedly cab-forward silhouette with an even briefer nose. It retained the quirky asymmetrical rear-wheel openings, but added dramatic plunging A-pillars to the profile.

If the design was breathtaking, so was the challenge to cash-strapped Lamborghini. Given the ambitious target, delivering this car within government regulations would be more difficult than bringing forth the Miura or Countach, but in April of 1987 Chrysler Corporation bought the Italian company. This event had many ramifications, not the least of which was that the vast technical power of a mass-market automaker was now available to the tiny band of Lamborghini craftsmen. No longer would Sant'Agata learn of the structural failure of chassis components only after production had begun. For the Diablo,

After years of turmoil, Chrysler, Lamborghini, and original designer Marcello Gandini finally agreed on a design for the Diablo (*bottom*). It was a completely new car with some familiar specifications—backward-mounted, mid-engine layout; transmission between the passengers; and rear-wheel drive. One conspicuous carry-over trademark was the scissor-wing doors (*top*).

Though the engine of the Diablo was still based on the Bizzarrini design dating back to the early '60s, almost everything about it was new. The biggest news was the increase in displacement and horsepower over the Countach. Outside, the Diablo sports stiffer aluminum-alloy panels. The final design of the engine cover (*top right*) was another change from the original Gandini design. It called for a fast-back panel at the rear, but the tunnel-roof design that appeared was used for better cooling and visibility.

Lamborghini could do structural engineering via finite-element analysis with the help of Chrysler's state-of-the-art super computers in Detroit.

Gandini's first design, however, was rejected by Chrysler soon after it took control. Gandini's revamp didn't quite make it either, and Lee Iacocca ordered in his U.S. styling staff. Under the direction of Tom Gale, Chrysler's vice president of product design, the Americans worked with Gandini on the final evolution. It proved a new way of doing things at the small boutique automaker. Whereas Gandini had drawn the Miura and Countach in an ad-lib stroke of genius, the Diablo was honed in the wind tunnel. It emerged with some of Gandini's creases planed away for a more organic look. The front spoiler was refined, the air intakes over the rear wheels were changed, and Gandini's original fast-back gave way to a tunnel-roof design for improved cooling and better visibility.

With Chrysler providing the technology and money, the Diablo was able to become a better car than the Countach ever could have hoped to be. On the Countach, body panels had to be flanged by hand. On the Diablo, they are shipped fully flanged and ready for installation. From the start, this eliminated considerable hand-fitting, improved the car's quality, and saved time. What was lost in Old-World technique was gained in uniformity and closer tolerances. Likewise, an in-

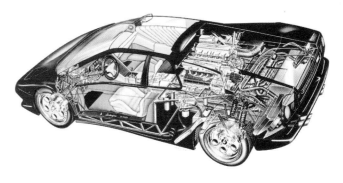

creased number of tooled pieces made the cabin substructure more sophisticated than the Countach's. Where the older car had aluminum patches to close gaps in the cockpit shell, Diablo has molded panels. Both are hidden from the eye by hand-stitched leather, but the Diablo's squeaks less.

Diablo's space-frame chassis is an evolution of the Countach's, but square- and rectangular-section steel tubes replace the Countach's round ones. The angled tubes are stronger and the flat surfaces are better for mounting components. A variety of

steel-alloy tubes, together with the aforementioned composites, helps the car exceed both American and European collision-impact standards. Parts of the front and rear structures are designed to crumple in an accident, creating crush zones. Lighter weight tubing in the front and rear was intentionally designed to absorb impact. Still other pieces of the chassis are grooved to direct the way they will bend in a collision.

For more durability outside, Diablo's doors and quarter panels are of a stouter aluminum alloy than the pliant

Exterior engine (*above*, and *above, left*) design was not as pretty as other Lamborghini motors, but power was incredible. Horsepower came in at 492 bhp and torque at 428 lbs/ft—improvements of 37 and 59 over the final Countach. Displacement was up to 5707 cc, and exhaust routed through catalytic converters, making the car's emission system legal in most of the world.

pure aluminum hung on the Countach. In addition, the pressed steel door frames and the steel roof are welded directly to the chassis, integrating the entire structure in the name of torsion-

In 1993 Lamborghini effectively replaced the base Diablo with a new model called the VT (*top* and *left*). This was the long-awaited four-wheel drive-version of the Diablo. Engine power was the same, but wheels were slightly larger at the rear and smaller in the front. The front wheels were now driven via a viscous coupling at the front of the transmission; 17 percent of the engine's power could be transferred in the event of rear wheel slip. Another advance over the base model was a new engine cover that nestled between the camshaft banks (*above*). This cover reduced noise in the interior of the car, helped clean up the engine design, and kept road debris off the engine.

The exterior of the Diablo VT was unchanged over the base model, but there were several new components inside. Electronically adjustable shock absorbers that could be set on automatic or manual were added. These new shocks grew firmer as speed increased, and lessened acceleration squat and brake dive.

al stiffness. Body rigidity is enhanced by the use of composite plastic panels in the center tunnel and in the passenger compartment. To keep weight down, composite materials developed by Lamborghini are used for the front decklid, the rocker panels, bumpers, spoilers, and engine cover. For a more uniform finish, the composite and metal panels are painted as a unit.

One element of the Countach that Lamborghini retained on the Diablo was the scissor-opening doors. The new car, however, has power-operated door windows that can be raised and lowered completely, unlike the half-panes on the Countach.

A 26.4-gallon fuel tank nestles behind Diablo's seats. Aluminum radiators are placed in the rear, at the extreme outboard edges of the car, and are mounted at roughly a 70-degree angle. It's easier to supply air to them there than to direct flow into the flanks just behind the cockpit, where the radiators in the Countach rested horizontally.

Diablo's competition-style four-wheel independent suspension uses upper and lower A-arms front and rear, coil springs, two tubular shocks in front and four in back, and anti-roll bars front and rear. Steering was initially manual rack and pinion, but after production began power assist was offered.

The 17-inch diameter O.Z. Racing three-piece aluminum wheels are evolutions of the 15-inchers introduced on the 25th Anniversary Countach. The fronts are 8.5 inches wide, the rears 13. Tires are special, hand-made Pirelli P Zeros—245/40ZR17 in front, 335/35ZR17 in back. A low-pressure warning system and a small can of compressed air substitute for a spare tire. Braking is done with massive ventilated discs; the fronts are 12.99 inches in diameter, the rears measure 11.2. Diablo does without an anti-lock system.

The Diablo is larger than the Countach in every way. Its 104.3-inch wheelbase is longer by 5.9 inches. At 175.6 inches in length, its body is longer by 10.2 inches. Overall beam is broader by 1.7 inches, at 80.3 inches, and with a

roof that is 43.5 inches off the pavement, Diablo is 1.8 inches taller than the Countach. The new car tips the scales at 3620 pounds, 170 more than the Countach. With driver aboard, Diablo has a front/rear weight split of 40/60, versus 42/58 on the Countach. Aerodynamically, the Diablo is far more efficient, its 0.30 coefficient of drag quite good in light of the airflow fight put up by the steamroller tires. By comparison, the Countach's 0.41 Cd. certainly held down top speed.

A lift of the engine cover reveals Diablo's 48-valve double-overhead cam aluminum V-12. Shouldering its big intake plenums with their 12 intake runners, it looks quite similar to the Countach's *Quattrovalvole*. Lamborghini has, in fact, extensively redesigned the Countach engine for the Diablo.

Displacement grows from 5.2 liters to 5.7. Bore and stroke increase, from 86 × 75mm (3.37 × 2.95 inches) to 87 × 80mm (3.39 × 3.12 inches)—a ratio more suitable to the displacement. The cylinders have pressed-in steel liners with Nikasil faces. Forged steel is used for the crankshaft and the connecting rods. Compression is up from 9.5:1 to 10.0:1. The intake manifold gets twin throttles for sharper response in all

running conditions. Single-row timing chains with dampers and an automatic tensioner system drive the dual overhead camshafts, replacing the Countach's manually adjusted double-row chains. Lubrication is by an integrated oil pump. The engine runs on unleaded premium fuel and routes its exhaust through catalytic converters, which are the standard now in Europe as well as the U.S.

Lamborghini has always regarded a car's engine as its soul, to be engineered with deference and assembled with respect, and this holds true for the Diablo. James D. Sawyer saw the new 5.7 under construction and recorded in *AutoWeek*, "The bottom of the V-12's aluminum heads are machined so precisely that even from six feet away you can see your face in them. Parts are weighed at the start of assembly to ensure that each engine is in balance. After assembly all engines are sent to a dyno room where they are run-in for two and a half hours."

Another area where the Diablo differs from the Countach is in electronic equipment. The principal advance is an up-to-date electronic engine-management system developed by Lamborghini and called *Lamborghini Injec-*

At the back, the fascia was revised to include the VT marker (*above*). Chrysler's biggest contribution to Lamborghini was the influx of cash and technology, but one edict that we can all be thankful for was the fact that every Diablo had to pass worldwide safety, emission, and noise standards. This ensured that the Diablo would come the United States.

tione Electronica (LIE). It has talents the Countach's single Marelli distributor could only dream about. LIE integrates the ignition and multipoint sequential fuel-injection systems for more exact engine control. Plus, it governs each cylinder bank individually.

All this helps put Diablo's V-12 at the very top of its class in muscle. The new engine makes 492 bhp at 6800 rpm—that's 37 more horsepower than the four-valve Countach's V-12 produced at its 7000-rpm peak. By comparison, Ferrari claims 478 horsepower for the F40's twin-turbo V-8 and 390 for Testarossa's flat-12. Diablo delivers 428 pounds/feet of torque at 5200 rpm, up from the Anniversary Countach's 369 pounds/feet at the same rpm. In addition to claiming a top speed higher than any of these rivals, Lamborghini credits Diablo with a time of 4.09 seconds 0-100 kph (0-62 mph). The Countach needed 4.7 seconds.

Moving all of this power to the rear wheels is a five-speed manual transmission. Marmiroli told *Car and Driver* that the Diablo eschews the six-speed gearboxes now fashionable because "with all the torque we have, a six-gear unit would add only weight and complexity." The final-drive ratio of the Diablo is 3.55:1, compared to Countach's 4.09:1.

As in the Countach, Diablo's power is fed forward through a single-plate dry clutch, then through the transmission, and back again via a driveshaft to the limited-slip differential. In the Countach, however, the driveshaft was routed through a passage in the engine oil sump. Diablo has the shaft alongside the engine to ready the powertrain for a four-wheel-drive model, the VT.

Lamborghini's plan for the Diablo called for major improvements in interior amenities and ergonomics. For this, Chrysler sent one of its designers, Bill Dayton, to take up residence in Italy and supervise design work on the passenger cell. The result is a thoroughly modern cockpit, with softer, rounded shapes replacing the Countach's squared edges. The center of the instrument panel slopes gracefully toward the windshield in a binnacle that holds controls for the climate system, stereo, and trip computer. There is a passenger-side grab bar on the right side of the dashboard.

Serving the driver is a steering column adjustable for height—as were columns on later Countachs—but it also telescopes 2.8 inches. Plus, the instrument cluster itself can be moved vertically about ½ inch. The designers thoughtfully kept the angle between the instruments and the horizon near zero for quicker, safer reads at triple-digit speeds. The seats recline and are again separated by a large center tunnel, on which sits a gated shift plate.

Automatic climate controls are standard, as is an Alpine sound system with a cassette or compact disc unit. Supplied with the car is a four-piece set of Italian-made luggage (retail value, about $3000) tailored to fit the five-square-foot cargo hold in the nose. As on the Countach, $5000 buys an ostentatious rear-wing spoiler of dubious aerodynamic benefit. Even more indulgent would be ordering the wind-up Breguet timepiece. That option costs $12,000. Still, all is relative, as the price of a Diablo is roughly $220,000.

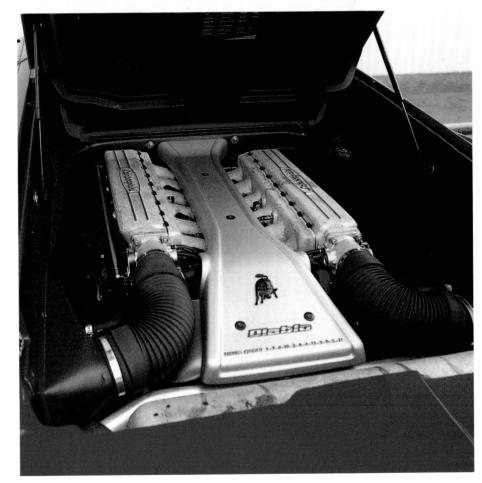

The interior of the VT was also substantially reworked (*top*). Most prominent were new gauges and instrument panel hood. Lamborghini also responded to criticism that the noise levels in the cabin were too high. Designers added extra sound insulation and a new engine cover (*above*) that went a long way to quiet things in back.

Sant'Agata started production in July 1990, building slowly to about 10 Diablos per week, for a goal of 500 annually. As of 1993 Lamborghini had built 350 Diablos. About 191 of those went to the U.S.

Despite its undeniable intervention, Chrysler seems well aware that it is but a neophyte in Lamborghini's exotic-car domain. At Diablo's debut, for example, Chrysler Vice Chairman Gerald Greenwald was measured about his company's part in it. "Chrysler played an important role in Diablo," he said, "but it was the role a good accompanist plays behind a virtuoso."

Gandini was displeased early on with the design changes wrought by Chrysler. However, he was present at their implementation, he posed with

the car at its introduction, and he did finally approve the use of his *disegno* signature on its flanks. When finally unveiled, the Diablo's styling garnered positive yet mixed reviews.

"It lacks the carnal, carnivorous presence that made its predecessor, the Countach, a favorite poster subject for feeding the fantasies of adolescents with rampant hormones," wrote James D. Sawyer in *AutoWeek*.

Jeff Karr in *Motor Trend* countered, "The visual impact is awesome. By comparison, the angular old Countach looks like it's mocked up out of cardboard boxes, and a Ferrari F40 looks like an injection-molded kid's toy."

"Say what you will about the styling of Lamborghini's new Diablo," concluded Giancarlo Perini in *Car and*

In 1993, about the same time Chrysler announced the sale of Lamborghini, a new model was revealed. The Diablo SE30 (*above*) was so named to mark the 30th anniversary of Lamborghini, but, unlike the mostly cosmetic 25th Anniversary Edition Countach, the SE30 was a very different car from the Diablo or Diablo VT.

Driver, "but when the car is coming straight at you, no shape is more arrogant, bold, and compelling.... The latest Lambo, as it snorts past, actually has the curious effect of causing passersby to hold their breath."

Driving one could have an alarming effect on respiration, as well. Just getting in is a chore. Press the shotgun-shell sized chrome button below the B-pillar to release the door, then lift the door by its edge. Negotiate the wide

sill and drop over the tall lower side bolsters into the firmly padded bucket seat. Once inside, shoulder room is adequate, but you'll be most comfortable if you're under six feet tall.

Overall ergonomics are an improvement over the Countach (and clearly influenced by Chrysler), but there are some problems. Deep in the footwell, the pedals crowd close enough to one another to cross-up footwork. More annoying, they're offset toward the center of the car to clear the suspension. At its lowest setting, the rim of the tilt steering wheel hides some of the gauges, and if you're long of leg, it won't adjust high enough to keep your knee, hands, and the center console from meeting during right turns. Reaching the controls for climate and stereo systems requires a stretch forward. If the day is warm, you might find that the air conditioner is insufficient in capacity and that there are too few dash vents to cool the cabin comfortably. Your view of the road ahead is excellent and if you adjust the power mirrors, visibility over the shoulders is adequate. Not much can be done about the view aft, however.

Sitting in the car is only half the experience—driving it is the other half. "The starter engages with a high-pitched metallic whine, and then the V-12 erupts into life with a deep bass thrum," wrote Nicholas Bissoon-Dath in *Car and Driver*. "It idles with the slightly uneven and temperamental flair of a thoroughbred, gently rocking the car as the revs rise and fall. Blip the throttle and the needle swings around the tach, accompanied by the *zizzing* of the cam chains; yet the revs die just as quickly after you lift off. This engine has a light flywheel."

The clutch pedal is heavy, the shift action is stiff, and the lever demands a firm hand to move it through the slotted gate. Despite a thick firewall that divides the engine bay from the cabin, the noise level is quite high, not noticeably diminished from the Countach. Unlike the Countach, which often stumbled at low speeds, Lamborghini's electronic engine controls keep the Diablo's V-12 tractable under virtually any condition.

"As the revs reach 7500, you shift into fifth and keep the pedal buried," relates Bissoon-Dath. "The car still surges forward with pure authority, and the road unreels before you like a videotape on fast forward. The speedometer keeps climbing: 175, 180, 185. As the speed fades, like exhaling a held breath, you find yourself smiling.... Driven hard, the Diablo simply obliterates traffic. It eats up gaps between cars in quick, effortless gulps."

Steering and handling are a different story. The wheel is alive in your hands. There is a lot of feedback from the road surface. Some describe the steering effort as meaty; others find it physically demanding. Even on center things are happening. The Diablo is far from ponderous, but it's so wide and you sit so low that it's difficult to anticipate the line through corners. Handling is typical of a high-powered mid-engine car. With so much mass in back, it wants to push the front tires through turns. Add more throttle—or lift off abruptly—and understeer quickly turns to oversteer.

"In every respect," Bissoon-Dath cautions, "the Lamborghini Diablo is a beast to be tamed. It requires a deliberate and firm hand, and it is a formidable machine that leaves those behind in amazement and awe. It may not be as civilized as an [Acura] NSX, but in terms of all-out performance it is a supercar of the very highest order. The king still reigns from Sant'Agata, and his name is Diablo."

In 1993 Lamborghini offered a four-wheel drive version called the Diablo VT. It takes its name from the viscous coupling at the heart of the all-wheel-drive system. When the rear tires begin to lose their grip because of road conditions or the amount of power being applied, the viscous coupling will automatically send up to 17 percent of the engine's torque to the front wheels until traction is restored. The system consists of the coupling itself, a carbon fiber forward drive shaft, a limited-slip front differential, and new front half-shafts.

The front and rear axle ratios have been selected so that the two spin at exactly the same speed. Then when the rears start to break loose, the viscous coupling locks up and transfers power to the fronts. This system is very efficient, lightweight and compact.

Also new on the VT are automatically adjustable shock absorbers. The shocks gain in firmness as speed increases or can be manually adjusted by the driver. The power steering that is optional on the base model is standard on the VT. All of this equipment adds about 110 pounds to the car's weight, so Lamborghini fitted stronger light-alloy Brembo calipers to increase stopping power.

Inside the cabin there are subtle refinements. The instrument cluster is lower. This was done to cut down on glare and ease readability. Minor revisions were made to the dash and passenger compartment and noise levels inside the cabin are reduced. One reason for this reduction is a new engine cover between the two banks of cylinders. This panel cleans up the engine compartment and protects the powerplant from road debris.

The price for the VT did not rise as much as some had suspected; in early 1994 it was a reasonable $239,000. Once

construction of the VT began, production of the regular Diablo was put on hold.

As if the VT weren't enough, Lamborghini decided to celebrate the company's 30th anniversary with a special Diablo model. Called the Diablo SE30, the new model will be produced in very limited numbers—only 150. The emphasis of the SE model is on light weight; in fact, the new model tips the scale at 3200 pounds, 420 pounds less than the rwd Diablo.

No area has been spared from the diet plan. Air conditioning, radio, cigarette lighter, electronic window lifts, and ashtray have been removed to lower weight. Lamborghini extensively redesigned the chassis and skin of the automobile to make use of light alloys and carbon fiber. The engine

cover was replaced with a louvered carbon-fiber panel that is not only lighter but more aerodynamic.

In the chassis, Lamborghini replaced the steel in the central tunnel with carbon fiber, and on the body, carbon composites have replaced aluminum and steel panels. New front and rear bumper panels are lighter and help promote downforce. The suspension has been augmented with light weight magnesium components and wheels. Disc brakes are drilled and the rear tires have increased in size.

Lamborghini spared no expense on the interior either. Racing-type carbon-fiber seats have replaced padded leather seats. In fact, all leather surfaces have been replaced with a lighter synthetic material. In the interest of safety, a central fire-extinguishing system

with fuel flow interrupt was added. Also, the front anti-roll bar is adjustable for stiffness from inside the cockpit.

Though the 25th Anniversary Countach was just a cosmetic package, Lamborghini decided that the SE would get engine improvements as well. Subtle but effective refinements to the engine management exhaust system have paid big dividends. While torque remains unchanged, horsepower is up to 525 bhp at 7000 rpm. Driver adjustable traction control was added and performance numbers are up in all categories. Top speed is up to 206 mph and the 0-60 time is at or below 4 seconds. Production for this model was scheduled to begin in June 1994 with a price of $255,000. Concurrent with the introduction of the SE30 model, *Auto-*

The SE30 was the hellacious side of the Diablo. Weight was reduced by every conceivable means and engine power was upped to 525 bhp. This gave the new car a 0-60 mph time of 4 seconds and a top speed of 206 mph. Carbon composites replaced most of the aluminum parts and a new rear panel improved aerodynamics (*left*). All leather was removed from the interior and carbon-fiber seats replaced padded buckets.

mobili Lamborghini SpA was in the midst of an owner change. Chrysler, unhappy with the declining fortunes of the Italian mark, put the company up for sale in the summer of 1993. They found a buyer in mid-November. Though the paperwork has yet to be finalized, it should be in the near future. The new owner, MegaTech Ltd., is actually a holding company 100 percent owned by SEDTCO Pty., an Indonesian conglomerate. This company also controls Vector Automotive Corporation—maker of the only true American super car. It will be interesting to see what, if anything, the union will bring. The new owners promise to allow Lamborghini to continue in its old traditions and maintain semi-autonomy.

Regardless, it's safe to say that everything produced at Sant'Agata Bolognese has been and will be formidable. One also could argue that precious few cars born there have enjoyed the symmetry founder Ferruccio Lamborghini held as his motoring ideal. It's a lofty goal, one few automobiles could satisfy. Lamborghini's car "without faults" would have to please both sides of his personality—the serious industrialist and the passionate enthusiast. On the surface, the Diablo doesn't seem to the be the kind of machine he had in mind, either. But the Diablo strikes a balance that Ferruccio himself embraces. It has that tribal rage.

"Refinement isn't on the Diablo's list of strengths, and neither is slavish attention to detail design," noted *Motor Trend*'s Karr. "In the grand and romantic tradition of the Italian Supercar, the Diablo is a thundering, fuel-sucking exercise in excess. As close to useless a car as you might ever hope to conceive. If that doesn't appeal to you on some level, strike some sort of cosmic chord in the back of your brain, then there's nothing I can say here that will make you understand."

model	1990-94 Diablo	1993-94 Diablo VT	1994 Diablo SE30
production	350 thru 1993	110 thru 1993	150 est.
engine	V-12	V-12	V-12
displacement cc/ci	5707/348	5707/348	5707/348
horsepower @ RPM (DIN)	492 @ 6800	492 @ 6800	525 @ 7000
torque @ RPM (lbs/ft)	428 @ 5200	428 @ 5200	428 @ 5200
length (mm/in.)	4502.6/175.6	4502.6/175.6	4502.6/175.6
width (mm/in.)	2059/80.3	2059/80.3	2059/80.3
height (mm/in.)	1115.4/43.5	1115.4/43.5	1115.4/43.5
wheelbase (mm/in.)	2674.4/104.3	2674.4/104.3	2674.4/104.3
track, front (mm/in.)	1523.1/59.4	1553.8/60.6	1523.1/59.4
track, rear (mm/in.)	1656.4/64.6	1656.4/64.6	1656.4/64.6
weight (kg/lbs)	1642/3062	1701/3750	1452/3200

INDEX